ADULT EDUCATION IN TRANSITION

A STUDY OF INSTITUTIONAL INSECURITY

BY
BURTON R. CLARK

UNIVERSITY OF CALIFORNIA PRESS
BERKELEY AND LOS ANGELES
1968

University of California Publications in Sociology and Social Institutions

THIRD PRINTING, 1968

University of California Press
Berkeley and Los Angeles
California

Cambridge University Press
London, England

ACKNOWLEDGMENTS

SEVERAL organizations and numerous individuals in sociology and education assisted in this study. The Social Science Research Council made possible full-time research for one year, 1952-53, through the provision of a predoctoral research training fellowship. The Los Angeles school system offered the specific opportunity for research by providing access to its personnel and records. To both organizations I am deeply grateful. It is a special pleasure to acknowledge the willingness of the personnel of the adult education branch of the Los Angeles system to undergo study by an outsider. Many others within and close to the California school system provided information and insight, and although they go unnamed their assistance was crucial in the research endeavor.

Among those in sociology who have had some contact with the study, I would like to acknowledge the assistance and criticism of Leonard Broom, Wendell Bell, Sheldon Messinger, and William S. Robinson. I am particularly indebted to Philip Selznick for assistance provided in various phases of the inquiry as well as for the analytical framework he has developed for the study of administration and institutional leadership.

This study is based upon a doctoral dissertation completed in the Department of Anthropology and Sociology, University of California, Los Angeles.

B. R. C.

CONTENTS

	PAGE
Introduction	43
I. The Background of Adult Education in California	47
Emergence of Adult Education	47
Development of Financial Support	51
II. Pressures on a Marginal Program	57
Marginality of Adult Education	57
The Enrollment Economy	61
Goals of Adult Education	63
III. The Adult School Organization in Los Angeles	67
Formal Structure	67
Student Clientele	72
The Teaching Force	86
The Administrators	105
IV. Service and Legitimacy	110
Cosponsoring Groups	110
The Need for Legitimacy	118
V. Continuing Insecurities	123
Attack from the Legislature	125
Competition from Community Colleges	130
VI. Implications for Theory and Policy	142
Institutional Change	143
Institutional Integrity	155
Policy Implications	157
Appendixes	
I. Methodology of the Research	165
II. Questionnaire on Teaching Staff	169
III. Socioeconomic Characteristics of Respondents to Questionnaire	174
IV. Additional Statistical Information on Questionnaire	177
V. Preliminary Registration Form	181
VI. Adult School Class Schedules	182
VII. The Problem of Course Classification	187
VIII. Organizations Cosponsoring Adult Classes	189

IX. Form Letter Used by a Cosponsoring Organization in
  Contacting Clientele 191
X. Excerpt from a Junior College Catalog 192

Bibliography 195
Index 201

INTRODUCTION

THIS sociological study of educational administration directly concerns the adult school in California and the way in which it has been shaped over the last quarter of a century as a definable and distinct type of public school enterprise. The inquiry is concerned with more than adult education, however; the research is guided by a broad sociological outlook, and it is intended that the study have meaning for both sociological theory and general educational policy. Some of the wider implications of this case study are explored at length in chapter vi. At this point, only a brief introductory statement of the orienting research framework is needed, in order to provide a background for the empirical materials that follow. What is the sociological rationale of this monograph and in what way is the inquiry related to problems in education?

In one sense this is a study in the sociology of formal organizations; in another, a study of an institution. In modern society, what occurs in various institutional systems is a matter of organizational action. Educational values are obviously implemented by school units; if we are concerned with why and how these values change, we must look to the organizations themselves and to their problems. With formal organization having become *the* tools of social action in large, complex societies, the study of institutional dynamics entails the way in which administrative branches are shaped and in turn affect the nature of an institution.

The sociological perspective[1] behind this inquiry has as a prime emphasis the analysis of organizational action as a way of understanding processes of institutional change. This orientation includes a search for the pressures upon organizations from within and outside their formal structures. It can be assumed that there are always conditions or forces in the environment of organizations to which they must adapt, with both anticipated and unanticipated, controlled and uncontrolled, consequences for institutional development. Operating pressures and administrative responses to them partly determine what can and will be accomplished. Organizational pressures may well be a prime determinant of institutional change. This sociological outlook, when applied to education, leads to a search for the basic pressures upon school administration. Organizations are seen whole, and in relation to their environmental conditions, their purposes, and their impact on social change. This is a simple statement of an elemental framework for in-

[1] See Philip Selznick, *Leadership in Administration*.

stitutional analysis, but it is sufficient to indicate an orientation little used in educational research. Organizational adaptation to environmental pressures is virtually an unexplored topic in education, and we have little systematic knowledge of the way in which the school as an organization shapes the institutional systems of which it is a part.

A rewarding feature of this general perspective is that it permits research on central problems of organizational leadership. In practice, leadership involves building and adjusting organizations to achieve certain purposes. Where we emphasize the *purposive* aspects of leadership, we ordinarily stress also the control of the means by which purpose is to be attained. But leadership is *adaptive* as well, in that purposes usually cannot be achieved unless the organization comes to terms with its environment. A major responsibility of leadership is the working out of satisfactory adjustments between organizations and environmental pressures. Administrators may find that they cannot control changes that are taking place in their organizations; or they may not even be aware of the long-run drift of affairs. Under more favorable conditions, the leaders may have considerable control over the way their organizations adapt and the consequences that ensue. The problem areas for investigation that follow from a broad sociological perspective on organizational action are of real concern to top administration. The exercise of leadership in education, as in other institutional areas, means facing the continuous problems of adjusting organizations and their purposes to environmental pressures, and of understanding and controlling the long-run effects of the adaptations that are made.

The adult school provides good case material for the analysis of institutional change in education. Along with junior college education, adult education is a recently developed public school program, having arisen mainly since World War I. Thus its historical development is somewhat more easily traced than is that of the elementary school or the high school. Also, adult education agencies are good subjects for research because they encounter severe problems of survival and security within the public school framework, and hence are likely to provide sharper, more dramatic examples of adaptation and its consequences. Since the adult education movement in the United States has been in business for about a quarter of a century, it is an interesting problem to investigate its institutional character as it has developed in the public school. Just what does the concept of adult education mean in a state school system of the United States in the middle of the twentieth century, and how is this meaning a product of history?

We can now specify the focus of the study. In what ways has adult education in California been shaped by the pressures to which it has been subjected over the last quarter of a century? How have its values been affected by practical matters of organizational existence? What special needs and problems have emerged within the adult-school organization that have been important in shaping its present character? What patterns of behavior and orientation are, in fact, its present defining features?

The general finding of the study is that the adult school in California has gradually taken on a service character: programs are highly adaptive to the expressed interests of students and community groups, and the schools are in close relationship to their clientele. With the schools "other-directed," the relation between students and the school is almost qualitatively different from the traditional modes. We shall find strong evidence of the service character of the schools in the way that classes are initiated and maintained, with students in effect making the final decisions. The service orientation is reflected also in the bases for hiring and firing teachers, in the duties of the administrative role, and in the content of administrative doctrines.

Another major area of the study lies in accounting for the reason for the emergence of this service character. For this purpose we must turn to the conditions under which the adult school has operated. Three factors are of basic importance: first, the marginal position of adult education within the public school system and the effect this status has upon the adult school; second, the nature of the purposes of adult education since the 1920's and its influence on the adaptive behavior of organizational leadership; and third, a specific set of operating pressures that stem from state legislation and problems of student clientele. The service institution identified in this study may be seen as a resultant of the conjunction of these conditions.

A short selective history is provided in chapter i. Chapter ii states the main state-wide conditions of administrative action. In chapters iii and iv, detailed empirical materials from the Los Angeles schools are presented, exhibiting the way in which policies and organizational attributes are related to the conditions previously specified. Chapter v considers the impact of the state legislature and the junior college upon the position and security of the adult school. The wider implications of the study are developed in chapter vi, and the methodology of the research is given in Appendix I.

CHAPTER I

THE BACKGROUND OF ADULT EDUCATION IN CALIFORNIA

SINCE the purpose of this study is to interpret an institutional evolution and not to write a history, a highly selective approach has been made to historical materials.[1] Two aspects of history are considered here: the early evolution of evening school purpose and activity toward adult education, and the growth of state aid for adult programs. These topics relate directly to the set of conditions (described in chap. ii) that have shaped public adult schools over the last quarter of a century. But before analyzing these environmental pressures, we must ask: What were the roots of adult education in California, and how did it acquire support as a public school program?

EMERGENCE OF ADULT EDUCATION

Evening classes began as early as 1856 in California and 1887 in Los Angeles.[2] Up until World War I, such classes were oriented in part toward adolescents, and the "proper" spheres of instruction were the ordinary vocational and academic curricula of the day schools. The first separate evening high school in Los Angeles, established in 1907, took the German continuation school as model, with part-time instruction provided for adolescents who had dropped out of school. Courses were for vocational-business training (e.g., mechanical drawing, patternmaking, bookkeeping) or the completion of elementary and high school requirements (e.g., United States history, arithmetic).[3] The small size of the Los Angeles evening schools in their earliest years, as compared to later expansion, may be seen in table 1.

In this early form the evening school was linked to elementary and secondary education by its programs. Some of the first evening schools were actually called boys' schools or girls' schools, with enrollment concentrated in pupils from twelve to sixteen years old. How early the evening school developed a distinctive program related to older adults is not readily determined from historical records, but the change was

[1] Descriptive historical material on adult education in California may be found in a number of sources, most of which are unpublished dissertations or Department of Education bulletins. The following are helpful sources, and provide references to the rest of the available literature: Lyman Bryson, *A State Plan for Adult Education*; Philip M. Ferguson, "Practices in the Administration of Adult Education in the Public Schools of California"; Joseph W. Getsinger, "The History of Adult Education in the Public Schools of California"; David L. MacKaye, "Problems Underlying the Administration of Adult Education in California."
[2] Getsinger, *op. cit.*, chap. iii.
[3] Los Angeles School System, *Board of Education Files*, Minutes, October 8, 1906.

[47]

under way by 1910. The night school moved into one category that was related to all adult age levels with the development of Americanization and citizenship classes (immigrant education) immediately before and

TABLE 1

SIZE OF ENROLLMENT, LOS ANGELES EVENING SCHOOLS

School year	Enrollment[a]	Population of Los Angeles City[b]	Ratio of enrollment to population
1887-88	30	......	....
1890-91	103	50,395	1:489
1895-96	145	......	....
1900-01	235	102,479	1:436
1905-06	298	....	....
1910-11	3,414	319,198	1:93
1915-16	22,080	....	....
1920-21	32,874	576,673	1:18
1925-26	64,980	....	....
1930-31	108,629	1,238,048	1:11
1935-36	85,557	....	....
1940-41	146,795	1,504,277	1:10
1945-46	118,821	....	....
1950-51	184,191	1,970,358	1:11

[a] SOURCE: Los Angeles Evening High School, *Statistical History of the Los Angeles City School District, Adult Education Program*, April 18, 1952. These figures are rough indices of the size of evening-school programs. Enrollment figures in adult education are simply head counts, with each student weighted equally. The number of hours spent in an adult school in a year, however, actually varies greatly from student to student, ranging from a few to hundreds of hours.
[b] SOURCE: U. S. Bureau of the Census, *Statistical Abstract of the United States, 1953*, p. 23.

during World War I. The growth of vocational training for adults as part of the war effort also brought in a large group of older students.[4] These two sources provided the night school with program elements distinctively related to an adult clientele.

Americanization and citizenship classes, in particular, had become by 1920 a special badge of merit of adult participation in the public school, for they were linked to a widespread concern during World War I over the assimilation of national minorities.[5] With this strong, if temporary, national urgency behind it, immigrant education played an important role in the evolution of evening-school functions, provid-

---

[4] Vocational training for adults was supported by the federal Smith-Hughes Act, passed in 1917, which provided federal aid to states for vocational education directors and classes on a matching-fund basis. This support contributed substantially to the traditional position of vocational education as the strongest component (in number of students) of American night schools.

[5] T. J. Woofter, Jr., "The Status of Racial and Ethnic Groups," in *Recent Social Trends in the United States*, pp. 585-586.

ing a public-supported bridge from the early continuation school, with its age-group limitations, to the expansions in purpose, program, and clientele that took place after 1920.⁶ At the level of belief and moral persuasion, the Americanization movement was a transition to the more general idea of educating older adults. The unassimilated (and later, the illiterate) within the adult population became approved bases for the schools. At the same time, with increasing participation of adults in vocational and academic courses, these too became approved means of growth.

Thus, from the early night schools for the young emerged schools for adults, centered on vocational training, Americanization and citizenship, and remedial academic education. Within adult education today, these tend to have the vestigial status of core areas, based on their early acceptance and their dominance until after 1925. But although they transformed the night school from the continuation school pattern, they soon proved to be inherently limited. All three areas together did not suffice to relate the evening school to major segments of the general public. Academic education never showed much promise in the evening school, for it faced the long-run trend of prolonged day schooling, and demand was lacking in the adult population. The Americanization clientele was limited to the national minority groups that could be reached successfully. After the restrictive national immigration legislation of the early 1920's, it was clear that Americanization was not a viable, permanent base for the schools.⁷ These tendencies provided an incentive for the evening school to seek new purposes and new programs.

A broadly stated philosophy, strongly voiced after 1925, provided the ideological room for growth. The advocacy of immigrant education changed into a plea for a wider adult education, an enlarged program relatable to the native population along many lines of interest. Adult education agencies began to emerge at local, state, and national levels; this common identification became known after 1926 as the adult education movement. Many specific events signified the change. The Department of Immigrant Education of the National Education Association

---

⁶ Morse A. Cartwright, *Ten Years of Adult Education*, p. 161.

⁷ "The increase in the number of classes and in enrollments can scarcely continue with the cutting down of immigration and the consequent small number of new arrivals from foreign countries.... The task of encouraging the establishment of night classes for foreigners in the cities of California is, therefore, completed, as there are no further possibilities of expanding into new places." Remarks made by director of the Department of Adult Education on the potentialities of immigrant education. State of California, Department of Education, *Thirty-second Biennial Report*, 1926, p. 64.

became the Department of Adult Education in 1924.⁸ The United States Office of Education took on an adult education specialist the following year.⁹ The American Association for Adult Education, initiated by Frederick Keppel of the Carnegie Corporation and supported by Carnegie funds, was set up in 1926.¹⁰ The A.A.A.E. included both school and nonschool agencies that were in any way related to the education of adults (e.g., libraries, museums, settlement houses).

While these changes were taking place in national organizations, a branch of the California State Department of Education was undergoing a similar redefinition. Immigrant education was first backed at the state level by an office of the State Commission of Immigration and Housing, beginning in 1915. This small unit was transferred to the State Department of Education as an Americanization desk in 1920, to better implement a state-wide Americanization and citizenship program. Along with the national trend, this office had become the Department of Adult Education by 1924.¹¹

The pronouncements on purpose made at this time emphasized that adult education, then a new term, was not to be restricted in either subject matter or clientele. This stress on vast potentialities was partly a reaction against the limitations of traditional patterns. In California the broadening of purpose was buttressed by the desire of state leaders to initiate and sustain liberal, cultural education. The head of the Department of Adult Education (Ethel Richardson) set forth a California Plan for Adult Education in 1926 that pressed for an inclusive program, with the accent on public affairs and discussion groups.¹² The California Association for Adult Education, a quasi-public organization directed by Lyman Bryson and closely linked to the state office, was set up in 1927 as a tool for getting this liberal education program off the ground.¹³ Despite the promotional efforts of Richardson and Bryson, however, local systems showed little tendency to develop this type of program under the adult education banner.¹⁴ Instead, the local tendency was to read an omnibus meaning into adult education. As we shall later see, the main consequence of broadening purpose was not a planned transformation of the evening schools into centers of adult liberal education, but consisted of "taking the wraps" off the schools. Here it

---

⁸ Andrew Hendrickson, *Trends in Public School Adult Education in Cities of the United States, 1929–1939*, pp. 14–15.
⁹ Getsinger, *op. cit.*, p. 9.
¹⁰ Cartwright, *op. cit.*, p. 17.
¹¹ *Thirty-first Biennial Report*, 1924, p. 37.
¹² MacKaye, *op. cit.*, pp. 16–19.
¹³ A review of the work of the California Association for Adult Education up to 1933 is contained in Bryson, *op. cit.*, *passim*.
¹⁴ MacKaye, *op. cit.*, pp. 21–22.

may simply be said the evolution was toward an open-ended program; later analysis will suggest the conditions and pressures that account for it.

To summarize the changes leading to the emergence of adult education: the first evening schools tended to be similar to continuation schools, concentrated on remedial functions, and were oriented toward out-of-school adolescents. Long restricted in program and clientele, these schools became predominantly related to adult students through the Americanization movement and the broadening of vocational education during and after World War I. These relatively restricted purposes then became enlarged into a broad social mission—adult education—in the 1920's. The philosophy which emerged at that time in grass-roots administration, and which dominates adult-school education today, emphasized the adoption of the entire adult population as potential students. This set of ideas will be systematically examined in chapter ii.

DEVELOPMENT OF FINANCIAL SUPPORT

The California public school system has achieved considerable autonomy from the rest of state and local government. At the local level, school districts have their own taxing power, and are governed by boards of education which may be either elective or appointive. Central municipal government generally has little control over school funds or school personnel. The districts are defined as part of a state structure, with lines of accountability extending directly from local school officials to county and state educational offices.

Local systems receive nearly all their revenue from two sources: their own tax levies and state apportionments. The state funds are determined by the state constitution and legislative enactment. Local districts usually receive between one-third and two-thirds of their total income from this source.[15] With the proportion of expenses covered by state monies related *inversely* to the share shouldered by local taxes, a central task of school management is the maximizing of income from state funds. State assistance is always of uppermost interest to board members and top administrators, and state appropriations frequently play an important role in determining local policy, operating as incentive for certain lines of action. Thus, while school districts have considerable autonomy *within* the state structure, local decisions

---

[15] In Los Angeles in 1952–53, 32.3 per cent of "general fund revenues" came from the state, 64.15 per cent from district taxes, and 3.55 per cent from other sources. Board of Education of the City of Los Angeles, *Controller's Annual Financial Report for the Fiscal Year Ending June 30, 1953*, p. vi.

may be guided by the flow of state aid. If the State Department of Education desires to unify small districts, it can exert pressure for unification by providing rewards in the annual apportionments. Or, if state officials wish to encourage a certain program, favorable financing provides a strong incentive for local systems to develop it. Within state systems, the expanding and contracting of financial aid is a basic means of influencing local districts. This point is especially relevant to adult education, for, as we shall later see, appropriations are strategic in such a marginal activity.

In 1903 the state of California set up a high school fund.[16] Five years later the state constitution was amended so that evening high schools were entitled to this support.[17] In 1911 the accounting unit for the apportionment of state funds was changed from "census children" to a measure based upon hours of actual attendance. The following year a decision of the State Supreme Court rendered this change applicable to evening high schools also. Thus, very early in the history of adult education in this country, local districts in California were receiving apportionment monies for evening-school attendance. The evening program, regardless of age of students, received financial support at approximately the same level as regular day programs. Such support would naturally augment any local incentive to develop evening high schools. The emergence and growth of this type of school after 1908 would suggest that state aid was crucial in its getting under way.[18]

State aid became a major stimulus for expansion of adult programs in 1921, when a special bonus was added for "the first thirty units of attendance."[19] This was in the period of strong interest in immigrant and literacy education, and the bonus was introduced in connection with a naturalization law.[20] Its effect upon the financing of adult classes was immediate and considerable. When added to regular apportionments, it covered program costs;[21] some districts were able to show a profit. The director of the Department of Adult Education stated:

> The law which provides for the financing of these classes is particularly well-planned. It provides for a bonus ... of $2,700 a year ... on the first thirty units

---

[16] *Thirty-third Biennial Report*, 1928, Part I, p. 25.
[17] *Ibid.*
[18] Cf. Getsinger, *op. cit.*, p. 72. Using Los Angeles as example, an evening high school established in 1907 was discontinued in 1908 for financial reasons, then reestablished in 1909. Two more evening high schools were added in 1912. Table 1 indicates the magnitude of growth after 1910.
[19] Assembly Bill 439, approved June 1, 1921, amending sec. 1761 of the *Political Code*. State of California, *Amendments to the School Law*, 1921.
[20] *Thirty-first Biennial Report*, 1924, p. 48.
[21] The 1921 bonus allotted $2,700 for the first thirty units of attendance in evening high schools and in special day and evening classes attached to day schools. Adult education attendance could, as a matter of administration and accounting,

of attendance. This is sufficient to pay the salary of the director and insure the district of enough state and county money to pay more than two-thirds and in most cases all of the cost of maintaining such classes.[22]

The 1921 law was so broadly worded that its program applicability was unlimited, since "nothing in the law confined the work to immigrants and the field spread into all areas where it could give service."[23] This bonus provided the financial stimulus for rapid expansion during the next decade. As one leader has explained:

> The generosity of the State has probably been the most potent cause for the organization of adult classes. High school principals, on proposing this organization to their boards of trustees, or city superintendents proposing it to the boards of education, are able to say that the entire support will be forthcoming without resort to local taxation.... In view of this, administrative boards were perhaps incurious, and certainly as the record of growth shows, were entirely agreeable to the organization of adult education as it exists. I have heard the same argument presented to community gatherings which might have been critical of the expense under any other condition.[24]

With state support at a high level, local programs expanded rapidly during the 1920's. Then, as an attempt to establish some administrative control over a scattered, uncoördinated development, a second bonus was added to the state structure in 1931. This was an administrative bonus granted to evening high schools for maintaining courses in a grades-sequence pattern similar to day schools, and for establishing separate administrative posts, positions not filled by day administrators.[25] Local districts were immediately stimulated to redefine their evening schools in order to qualify for state funds, providing a good example of the way in which appropriations can determine local action. The effect of this bonus may be seen in table 2. Of the sixty evening schools in the state in 1930–31, only nine, or 15.0 per cent, maintained grades. Within one year some sixty-eight schools, or 86.1 per cent, had formally assumed this status. Thus a change in the system of state appropriations brought quick local action. However, this was merely a

---

be parceled out in small blocs to a large number of schools within one school system. One researcher has shown that this bonus amounted to over $180,000 in one year (1937–38) in Los Angeles, with adult education receiving state support at the rate of $127.79 per average daily attendance, compared to $85.50 for the regular high school. At that time the Los Angeles adult program was 90–100 per cent supported by state funds. Ruth E. Meilandt, *A Study of the Adult Education Program of the Los Angeles City High School District*, pp. 32–34.

[22] *Thirty-first Biennial Report*, 1924, p. 48.
[23] David L. MacKaye, "Aims and Purposes of Adult Education in California," *Adult Education Bulletin*, 9 (October, 1944), p. 11.
[24] MacKaye, "Problems Underlying the Administration of Adult Education in California," p. 31.
[25] State of California, Department of Education, *Bulletin*, no. 4 (1932), Part I, p. 6.

change in labels, for the most part, and did not bring state administrative control. As a matter of formal requirement, some courses were classified into a grades-maintained scheme. But only a few classes had to be treated in this way, and liberal definitions of classes appropriate for high school credit were permitted. The importance of the change lay in its adding a second bonus to the system of financial incentives and in the impetus it gave to the rise of a separate group of administrators.

TABLE 2

CHANGES IN FORMAL STATUS OF EVENING HIGH SCHOOLS IN CALIFORNIA

Evening high schools maintaining grades	Number of schools	
	1930-31	1931-32
Grades 9-10	1	2
Grades 9-11	2	1
Grades 9-12	6	63
Grades 10-12	0	1
Grades 9-14	0	1
Total number maintaining grades	9 (15.0%)	68 (86.1%)
Number with *no* grades maintained	51 (85.0%)	11 (13.9%)
Total number of evening high schools	60 (100.0%)	79 (100.0%)

SOURCE: State of California, Department of Education, *Biennial Report*, 1932, Part I, p. 27.

The next important change affecting the adult program came in 1945. The "first thirty units" bonus of 1921 was repealed, but in return the apportionment unit was redefined so as to be more favorable to local districts. Average daily attendance (A.D.A.) for adult education was changed from a four-hour day to a three-hour day. This three-hour unit, as the basis for calculating state apportionments, increased a district's revenue for its adult program by one-third for any given number of attendance hours. Since the junior colleges were on a three-hour day, while elementary and high schools were on a four-hour basis, the change actually placed adult education on a higher financial base than the elementary and high school programs and on a par with the junior colleges. Thus adult schools were in a favorable position with respect to the competition then emerging from the junior colleges. (See chap. v.) In terms of financial incentives, however, the 1945 change simply took away a special type of bonus and provided another latent one that became an integral part of the apportionment system.

This change was followed two years later by the most important change of all—a modification in school finance that had major consequences for adult education. An equalization formula was added to the school financial structure in 1947 in order to provide additional state aid for poor school districts. The state determines which districts have the greater financial burden per child, by comparing district attendance figures against taxable assessed wealth. How much equalization money, if any, a district will receive in addition to its basic aid is determined by its relative position in the equalization formula. The gaining of equalization funds hinges on the ratio between attendance and district wealth. Increased enrollment makes a district poorer: it dilutes the assessed valuation behind each unit of average daily attendance, increasing the strain on the local tax levy.

The special consequence this formula had for adult education comes from the fact that adult education funds are handled within the financing of high school or junior college districts. Adult attendance is part of the reportable attendance of these units. Districts become "poorer," according to the equalization formula, by increasing the size of their adult programs. The attendance population of a high school district can be rapidly expanded in this fashion. With the limits on day-school enrollment set by the demographic characteristics of the general population and by the efficiency of truant officers, the main potential for rapid expansion in enrollment, and thus in income, often lies in adult education. With more adult classes, a district may, for example, increase its returns from $100 to $110 or $120 per A.D.A. The increased return is applicable to *all* attendance of the district, and not just to the adult education units.

In this way an enlarged adult education program became, after 1947, a basic means of increasing district revenues. This was least true for wealthy systems which did not participate in equalization funds; it had little direct effect in Los Angeles. But for districts already receiving some equalization aid, or near the point of eligibility, the income potential of adult education became a major incentive for its rapid expansion. It is "efficient" school management for local administrators to attempt to increase and maximize returns under the state formula.

This effect of adult education upon equalization funds seems not to have been anticipated by the state legislature and by many educators. The objective result of the 1947 legislation, however, was to provide a new high point in appropriation-induced motivation throughout the state. The budget value of adult education to local systems was enhanced and the outlay for the program was doubled in the period 1947–

1952.²⁶ In 1952–53 the state financial structure for adult education was composed of the basic aid to all districts, figured on average daily attendance ($90 per A.D.A.); the 1931 administrative bonus for each approved evening school (totaling $4,000 per school in 1952–53); and additional equalization returns in some school districts. The last two aspects of the structure simply accentuate the motivational consequences of the first component, the attendance basis for apportionments. In chapters ii and iii we shall discuss state finance in terms of budget pressures upon school administration without further mention of specific measures.

It is to this financial base that educators have reference when they speak of the early and generous support that was responsible for the growth of adult education in California.²⁷ State support was established as early as 1907 for evening schools; it became a major incentive for expansion in 1921, with a special bonus for adult classes; it was reënforced with a second bonus in 1931; and state aid became a special prize for equalization districts after 1947. For a program that has not been a central school activity, these state measures have played a key role. The appropriation system relates to local decision-making in ways that must be understood and taken into account in interpreting institutional processes in this adult education context.

---

²⁶ State of California, *Partial Report of the Senate Interim Committee on Adult Education*, 1953, p. 444.

²⁷ Homer Kempfer (Adult Education Specialist, United States Office of Education), "State Programs of General Adult Education," *Adult Education Journal*, 7 (April, 1948), pp. 75–81. Kempfer's survey figures for 1946–47 show that twenty-one states provided some state aid for adult education. Four states used an attendance basis for computing apportionments. California had the most extensive program, owing to "favorable financial provisions, an early start, substantial State Department leadership, and a liberal interpretation of adult education."

Chapter II
PRESSURES ON A MARGINAL PROGRAM

THE THEME of this study is the emergence of service organizations in adult education in California. Some of the characteristics of this type of organization are later developed in chapters iii to v. The purpose here is to present the historical conditions that have determined the adult school. These conditions have been reconstructed in analysis from the experience of participants, and especially from the historical record contained in organizational files, public documents, and previous studies. Here, as throughout the report, documentation is drawn only from materials that are already available to the public.

The three elements discussed below are defined as conditions of administrative action. For a quarter of a century they have defined the environment within which administrators have had to make decisions. Over the long run, it is possible for the administrators to modify the conditions; for example, through sustained effort, to reduce the marginal position of adult education. But in the here-and-now of administrative decisions, these historical elements are conditions of action rather than means or ends readily changed by the individual administrator.[1]

MARGINALITY OF ADULT EDUCATION

In broad terms, the primary mission of a public school system in the United States is the education of the young. Different school levels are accepted as legitimate concerns of tax-supported education on the basis of their part in the grades progression. Historically, public responsibility for elementary education was established in the nineteenth century, and public high schools won acceptance during the first quarter of the twentieth century. In California, junior colleges have become widespread in the last twenty-five years, with a state system of more than sixty colleges. They are closely linked to the grades-sequence structure, since they provide the thirteenth and fourteenth years, and sometimes grades ten to fourteen.[2] Their existence is strongly guaranteed, although their ultimate character is somewhat in doubt. In higher education, California also has a system of state colleges under the State

---
[1] This point is emphasized here, since the goals of adult education are treated as a condition of local decision-making. Compare the view of Chester I. Barnard on purpose as part of the objective environment within which new decisions are made: *The Functions of the Executive*, chap. xiii.

[2] In California, public junior colleges are defined as an upward extension of secondary education. See Jesse P. Bogue, *The Community College*, pp. 9–14.

Board of Education, and the University of California under an autonomous Board of Regents.

In contrast to elementary, high school, and junior college education, the adult program is a separate, peripheral activity, and its clientele is completely outside the compulsory-attendance age groups.[3] When an adult program is initiated, it must make its way within a family of established programs, contending with the strong, central departments for budget support and favorable treatment. Since its inception, adult education has been, and to some extent still is, a marginal program within the school system. It is difficult to assess organizational marginality precisely, since it depends upon the degree of acceptance afforded a program by different groups within and outside the school system. As evidence, however, we may note some symptoms of the peripheral status in which the adult schools have operated.

1. Some evidence of marginality is indicated in the constitutional status of adult education. The state school system is composed of elementary, high school, and junior college districts; these are the basic legal units for finance and administration. Once voted into existence by the local electorate, these districts, under their respective boards of education, must maintain appropriate schools. In contrast, adult education does not have a district status, and adult classes must be attached to the basic legal units. Also, adult education is backed mainly by permissive legislation; the state authorizes adult classes, but makes no mandate for them. Classes in citizenship and literacy are the main exceptions to this nonmandatory status.[4]

2. As frequently happens with a new activity, adult education began as a secondary responsibility of administrators working with other programs. The administration of adult education in the state had this character until 1931, and it was symptomatic of the program's second-class position. After 1931 there were separate principals, but mainly in part-time posts. The number of full-time positions has gradually increased, but it is only within recent years that the largest department in the state, for example, has been manned completely by full-time administrators (the adult education branch of the Los Angeles school system in 1947–48). Part-time administration has been a contributing factor to, as well as a symptom of, a marginal position. This index suggests that marginality has been partially reduced during the last twenty-five years.

---

[3] Full-time attendance is compulsory until the age of sixteen in California. If a person drops out of school after that age and has not graduated from high school, he must attend a continuation school for four hours a week until he is eighteen. Continuation schools are not now considered a part of adult education. State of California, *Education Code*, 1953, secs. 16601, 17001.

[4] *Ibid.*, secs. 9051, 9094.

3. A third symptom of marginality is the absence of separate plant facilities and other fixed capital. If adult education were a basic purpose of the schools, with a status approximating that of other levels, it would possess special facilities. If a comparison is made to the junior college,[5] the loss in organizational stability is apparent. Once a school system has equipped a junior college with classrooms, machine shop, library, and football stadium, there is a reasonable guaranty that it will remain. The adult school, in contrast, has no physical roots with which to protect itself against retrenchment; it can more readily be consolidated or discontinued. Moreover, plant facilities must be used that are not easily adapted to adult use. Classes are held in elementary and high school rooms or at branches located on nonschool properties. The adult administrators seek separate facilities, but they have little chance of obtaining them from public funds. Thus it becomes a struggle to obtain even small wooden bungalows on school property for the sole use of adult classes in Los Angeles.

4. The pressure of economy-minded interest groups is especially severe upon the adult school. (See chap. v.) The recommendations of such groups take a special programmatic bent in adult education. Whereas economy drives aimed at the other school levels center on plant expansion and teachers' salaries, in adult education the main issue is curtailing content and clientele. Major segments of the program are not accepted by the watchdog economy groups, who seek to abolish them. The fact that the work of the adult administrators is sharply questioned indicates low acceptance by strong outside groups.

5. The most important symptom of the present marginality of the adult school is the necessity of having to sell the program to the public and especially to other educators. This need is strongly felt within the ranks of the Los Angeles adult administrators. It stands out in the reports of such state-wide groups as the California Association of Adult Education Administrators and in the bulletins of the Bureau of Adult Education of the California State Department of Education.[6] The administrators define their position as "stepchild" in nature. They perceive that they are not afforded a fundamental acceptance by other schoolmen and by state legislators.

[5] Comparisons with junior colleges are particularly useful, since adult education and junior college education are the younger school programs. High schools began to push upward into the thirteenth and fourteenth years about 1907; separate junior colleges were authorized, with state support, in 1921. Their initial expansion thus began in approximately the same era as that of the adult schools. State of California, Department of Education, *Thirty-third Biennial Report*, 1928, Part I, pp. 27–29.

[6] State of California, Department of Education, Bureau of Adult Education, *Report and Proceedings of the Montecito Workshop in Adult Education*, 1952, pp. 80–89.

> ...the adult program should ... be accepted ... as an equal partner when it comes to the status of its administrator, the pay of its teachers, use of facilities and so on. This equality should be thoroughgoing and sweep away the various forms of second-class treatment of adult educators and their students which are still found in many districts. Members of governing boards, superintendents, and day school administrators and teachers ... tend to tolerate or show condescension toward adult programs as though they were step-children in the family of public schools, taken in for their subsistence allowances rather than for themselves.[7]

To the extent that the program's educational value is ranked low relative to other uses of school funds, the position of the adult school is insecure. *Organizational marginality is the basic source of insecurity* for the administrative branches of adult education. The long-term problem of adult-school administrators is to achieve a "peer" position. They badly need a parity level, clearly defined and respected by all. The search for acceptance is a struggle for security.

6. Since adult education is financed within high school and junior college districts, much of its budgetary support has been derivative and often unanticipated. The amount of state aid is an ambiguous index of program marginality. The early bonuses for adult education were indicative of little local support and reflect the attempts of state authorities to back the program. In the face of local marginality, generous state aid has been a strong prop. This suggests a hypothetical index. One real test of program strength would be the scaling down of state aid to the same proportion allotted to other programs. The reduction would force local boards to assess program value. A real test is not likely to happen in a clear-cut way, but posing it as a hypothetical test is useful. Both advocates and opponents of the present program agree that fundamental changes would be made. Opponents have sought to limit state aid for certain types of classes, knowing that local boards would not support these classes out of local taxes. Adult educators, on the other hand, have feared and fought such changes. The existing program could not maintain itself in its present form if its budget value were reduced. Since state aid may be modified from year to year, adult administrators are always faced with the possibility of an adverse change.

It seems evident that security for the adult school is dependent upon the acceptance, principally by those with power within school ranks, of adult education as a central activity of the public school, or, minimally, acceptance at a well-defined, stabilized parity level. That this position has not been achieved is reasonably clear to both participants and observers.

---

[7] *Ibid.*, pp. 80–81.

THE ENROLLMENT ECONOMY

The legislation outlined in chapter i determines the allotment of state funds. State aid for a year is set by the attendance recorded during the preceding year. The larger the sum of attendance hours added by adult education to the school district within which it is reported, the greater the district's revenues from the state the following year. With this apportionment base, it is not surprising that administrators take cognizance of the close relationship between attendance, state funds, and local funds. The incentives of the state funds in decision-making pivot on the fact that the local share of expenses is small where costs are well covered by state aid. State support is at a high ratio when class attendance is large. This is always true when district income from the state is figured on an attendance basis. For while *income* varies with attendance, the *cost* of classes is relatively fixed. It is set mainly by teachers' pay, administrative salaries, and plant upkeep, which do not vary according to class size. If, for example, the pay rate for adult-school teachers is $5.50 an hour, class expense is pegged at this level whether the class has fourteen students or fifty. But with a turnout of fourteen the local district must pay more than half of class costs, whereas the class of fifty more than pays for itself out of state reimbursements.[8]

The close relationship of cost to attendance determines the enrollment pressures upon the personnel of the adult school. These may be termed budget pressures: the cost-attendance relationship forces administrators to maintain and build attendance because of its import for school income. The state provisions set incentives for local action in the direction of attendance building. Even for districts which do not participate in equalization funds, the attendance-cost relationship shapes policy. In most districts, school authorities are reluctant to use local revenues to support the adult program.[9] Especially in districts where the school budget is extremely tight, the elementary and high school units have priority upon scarce funds. Then, in equalization districts, the cost-attendance relationship motivates local administrators to profit

---

[8] In the Los Angeles adult schools in 1952–53, the hourly pay rate for teachers was $5.25, $5.50, and $5.75 an hour, depending on years of service (first year, second year, three years or more). State apportionments based on average daily attendance were approximately 18 cents per hour of student attendance ($95 per A.D.A., divided by 525 hours, the number of hours in one unit of A.D.A.). Thus thirty students would about cover the cost of a teacher receiving $5.50 an hour.

[9] Compare the judgment of the Strayer Report: "In practice, it is the exceptional district that uses a substantial amount of local funds to support classes for adults." Committee on the Conduct of the Study of Higher Education in California, *A Report of a Survey of the Needs of California in Higher Education*, March 1, 1948, p. 49.

on the program and use the surplus revenues for other departments. It is a matter of record and of common knowledge within administrative ranks that this has occurred in many school districts."

One other main condition determines that attendance problems will sharply affect adult schools—the nature of the student body. These schools have no assured public; student participation is always voluntary. Furthermore, attendance is a supplementary, part-time interest; rarely does it represent a primary commitment of time and effort. All school levels with students above the compulsory attendance age face the problem of voluntary students who may withdraw, but in no other program is this problem so acute

These conditions define a prime organizational problem of gaining a student body. Adult schools must create clienteles. To survive and prosper they must so adapt to the environment that they are reasonably guaranteed an aggregate of students at any one time. The problem is threefold: out of the general population, students must be pulled to the adult schools; the organization must then hold them in attendance; or, where students fall away, the schools must replace them. The possibility of losing large blocs of voluntary students is always a threat. The survival of individual positions and the strength of the entire organization depends entirely upon success in recruiting and holding student bodies. The impact of attendance upon organizational strength is increased where adult education is financed as in California. With the attendance-cost factor operating in the face of voluntary student ties, the solving of enrollment and attendance problems must take first place in administrative action. This confluence of budget pressures with the nature of the clientele is here termed the *enrollment economy*. It is suggested that the enrollment economy constitutes the basic complex of pressures operating upon the adult school. This is because organizational needs for survival and security are distinctly shaped in the adult education context by these factors.

To comprehend its potential impact, the enrollment economy should be seen in relation to other conditions. The peripheral status of the adult school is very important: the greater the marginality, the stronger is the pressure of the enrollment economy. School systems will not contribute generously to a program they only weakly accept; program administrators who are insecure because of marginal status are more susceptible to the pressures upon them.

Purpose plays a significant role in relation to operating pressures. In

---

[10] State of California, *Partial Report of the Senate Interim Committee on Adult Education*, 1953, pp. 27–33, 107–112.

the following section, the manifest goals of adult education are analyzed. This discussion will then provide us with a configuration of three historical conditions: the marginality of organizational activity, the pressures of the enrollment economy, and the potential effect of stated purpose.

GOALS OF ADULT EDUCATION

The philosophy of adult education that was prevalent in the late 1920's provided a liberal interpretation of program boundaries. In the pronouncements of state and national leaders, purpose was broadened to include a wide range of adult interests. Moreover, these general views of purpose were adopted by individual schools as their own ends. As many observers have noted, organizations usually make general formulations of the ends toward which they are striving, with formally stated goals ambiguous enough to permit a wide range of interpretation.[11] The administrative branches of adult education in California relate themselves to very ambiguous ends, with goals so defined that they include all adult learning. A brief analysis of these objectives may reveal their potential relevance for administrative decision-making.

The following statements were taken from a 1951 bulletin of the California State Department of Education, and were selected because they represent a consensus among the adult administrators of the state and are supported by the California Association of Adult Education Administrators. Assertions published in state bulletins are not likely to be "merely" public relations, since the bulletins are read mainly by school personnel. The general purposes of adult education are stated as follows:

> Adult education embraces the learning achieved by adults during their mature years. It is new learning, not just a continuation of learning. The major purposes of adult education are, first, to make adults in the community aware of individual and community needs, and, second, to give such education as will enable them to meet problems that exist now. Adult education stems directly from the people. The curriculum is based on present needs and problems.
>
> Education for the solution of problems in a democratic society includes the total range of human learning, from the learning of the simple means of communication, reading and writing, to the actual solution of the most complicated problems of human relations.[12]

Such general terms as "the learning achieved by adults during their mature years," "individual and community needs," "the total range of

---

[11] Compare the discussion of the formal purpose of the business firm, and especially of the labor union, in Arthur M. Ross, *Trade Union Wage Policy*, pp. 24–27.
[12] State of California, Department of Education, *Bulletin*, 20 (May, 1951), p. 2.

human learning" are widely used in expressions of adult education philosophy. The phraseology suggests that the program ought to be extremely diversified in order to meet a host of problems. This diversification is to be "based on present needs and problems" of the adult population.

The ambiguity of such statements usually presses for more specific objectives. "Major purposes" hardly constitute a stated mission from which directives for action can be deduced. The philosophy remains isolated from the world of its implementation unless it can be made more specific. The need for formulating a set of goals is much discussed, and occasionally the more general statements are challenged as meaningless, usually by program critics but sometimes by "friends of adult education" and by administrators themselves. Declarations of general purpose are usually followed by lists of objectives. To continue with the same example, the quotation is followed by this statement:

Seven specific objectives of adult education in California may be stated as follows:

1. To make adults aware of their civic responsibilities to one another and to the community.
2. To make them economically more efficient.
3. To develop an understanding of the attitudes and personal adjustments required for successful home life and family relationships.
4. To promote health and physical fitness.
5. To provide an opportunity for cultural development.
6. To supplement and broaden educational backgrounds.
7. To provide for the development of avocational interests through opportunities for self-expression.[12]

These objectives reaffirm the generality of organizational purpose. Although the sub-objectives ostensibly pinpoint the intent, the categories themselves are ambiguous, and include all potential subjects and practices. Their open-ended character suggests that they are not likely to establish limitations on practice, especially in view of the fact that the specific objectives do not receive differential emphasis or priority. These statements, as well as the declarations of general purpose, give formal approval to *all* courses, since a rationale for any class could be worked out from one of the categories. "Cultural development," "self-expression," and so on cover all possibilities, and each class is a means of achieving one or more of these ends. The objectives are likely to be an administrative rationale for programs highly flexible in content and

---
[12] *Ibid.*

administration. The formal goals seem to add up to program diversification as the basic purpose of the schools.

The ends of action are directly related to administrative behavior so far as they have some bearing upon the desirability of choosing one path rather than another. To have impact on decisions, goals must provide criteria of what should be done; or must be connected to more specific goals (a means-ends chain) that provide cues for behavior; or must be bound to traditional standards of conduct. The goals must have a content relevant to choice if they are to guide decisions. The more diffused the goals of an organization, however, the less chance that they will intervene in decision-making. If they are very broad, they may not have any influence at all on decisions, for example, in regard to what courses should be instituted. If the objectives amount to program diversification, it is clear that the manifest goals provide the administrator with open-ended choices. The possibilities among which choice must be made are equally valid in the light of stated purpose.

This logical analysis suggests that adult education programs of the California schools are likely to be weak in purpose, in the sense that decision-making criteria cannot flow from stated goals. This means that the criteria for decision-making will come from the day-to-day pressures of the enrollment economy. In this relationship of formal goals to operating pressures, the stated ends apparently do not counter the demands of the enrollment economy. In fact, there seems to be a strong congruence between enrollment needs and the possible outcome of the diffuse goals in action. The organizational objectives set wide limits for adjustment to operating pressures. How these pressures work out in organizational policy, and the meaning of the stated ends as an administrative rationale, will become clearer as the report progresses.

In summary, the diffuse goals of adult education are not likely to control decision-making. Their generality widens the discretion of program administrators. In the context of the enrollment economy pressures, where organizational survival and security depend upon the solving of attendance problems, the day-to-day interpretation of such open-ended purpose is likely to be shaped by these solutions. And, in the context of marginality, it is even more likely that basic organizational needs will rule the day.

As the most significant factors in the environment of decision-making, the three conditions specified in this chapter may be viewed as underlying the development of the adult school in California. These abstracted elements do not determine all facets of organizational behavior, but they distinctly and importantly shape orientation, motivation, and action. If an interpretation centered on these three factors is meaningful, it should allow us to tie together and explain core features of a program in a particular school system. The relation of an adult education department to its own personnel and students, to other school departments, and to groups in the community should be relatable to the interpretative theme. As case material, we shall examine adult education policies and procedures of the Los Angeles school system..

CHAPTER III

THE ADULT SCHOOL ORGANIZATION IN LOS ANGELES

THE MATERIAL in this chapter is centered on policies and procedures that affect student clientele and teaching personnel. These two areas are explored in the latter part of the chapter. First, however, a description of the formal structure of the school system will provide the organizational setting of the adult education branch.[1] The relationships between this branch and other departments are brought out at appropriate points in the later analysis.

FORMAL STRUCTURE

The Los Angeles city school system, in keeping with the character of the city, is spread over an enormous territory. In 1952 it embraced 827 square miles, or four-fifths the area of Rhode Island.[2] The total organization consisted of about 450 schools, with some 22,000 teachers and classified employees, and a student population of more than 400,000.[3] In its territorial jurisdiction, budget, and organization, the school system is indeed a big business.

In internal arrangement the school system has three principal components (see chart 1): the divisions of Elementary Education, of Secondary Education, and of Extension and Higher Education. Each division has a headquarters office with an associate superintendent in charge. The elementary division is broken down into five districts. These geographically dispersed offices are headed by assistant superintendents, with about three hundred sixty elementary schools under their jurisdiction. The elementary level is the only one in which there is a geographic breakdown of overhead units (e.g., the district offices). The Division of Secondary Education has, as important substructures, junior high and senior high branches, each with an office in central headquarters topped by an assistant superintendent. There are forty junior high schools and forty senior high schools below these two offices in the chain of command. The third major unit, the Division of Exten-

---

[1] For discussions of the concept of formal structure see F. J. Roethlisberger and William J. Dickson, *Management and the Worker*, chaps. xxiii–xxiv; Herbert A. Simon, D. W. Smithburg, and V. A. Thompson, *Public Administration*, pp. 79–91; Philip Selznick, "Foundations of the Theory of Organization," *American Sociological Review*, 13 (1948), pp. 25–35; Francis G. Cornell, "Administrative Organization as Social Structure," *Progressive Education*, 30, no. 2 (November, 1952), pp. 29–35.

[2] Los Angeles City School Districts, Office of Public Information, *Saludos Amigos*, March, 1952.

[3] *Ibid.*

[67]

sion and Higher Education, has two main substructures, each with a headquarters office: the junior college central office, with an assistant superintendent; and the adult education branch, headed by a supervisor. Junior college directors and adult school principals are formally responsible to these two administrators.

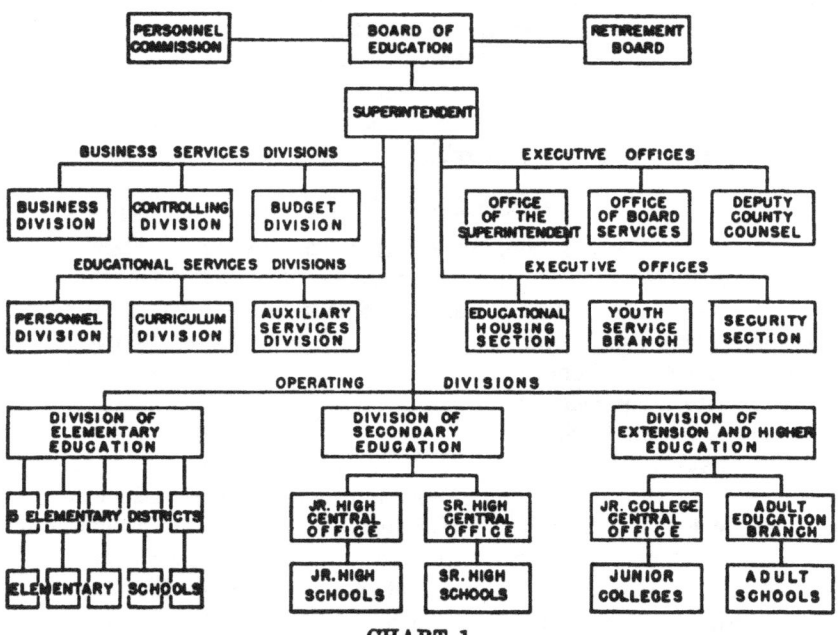

CHART 1

ORGANIZATIONAL STRUCTURE OF THE LOS ANGELES SCHOOL SYSTEM, 1952–53

SOURCE: Adapted from chart of Los Angeles school system in use 1952–53 (no date).

These line divisions are supplemented by numerous headquarters offices that have proliferated in the school system's rapid growth. These units are grouped in chart 1, again using the nomenclature of the school system, as educational services divisions (personnel, curriculum, and auxiliary services), business services divisions (budget, business, and controlling), and executive offices (superintendent, office of board services, deputy county counsel, educational housing section, youth services branch, and security section). The educational services divisions are headed by associate and assistant superintendents, with an additional assistant in curriculum. The budget division, a business office quite important in its relationship to the operating divisions, has an associate superintendent; the office of board services is staffed with an associate superintendent operating as secretary to the board of education; and, within the office of the superintendent, an assistant superintendent is in charge of school defense. Thus, in 1952-53, the formal structure of headquarters, together with the five elementary district offices, included a superintendent, seven associate superintendents, eleven assistant superintendents, a business manager, and a controller. The professional staff of headquarters (including the elementary district offices) totaled two hundred sixty. Below the superintendents are supervisors, consultants, and coördinators. This staff comprises an administrative superstructure above the administrative personnel of the individual schools and colleges.

In their formally constituted positions, the numerous division chiefs are responsible directly to the superintendent. (See the lines of command in chart 1.) This is a complicated organization; and the formal structure shown in organizational charts has been supplemented by permanent coördinating units. The superintendent and the division chiefs have been organized in a division heads council, the top policy-making body among the professional administrators. The council seems to be a working part of the formal system. It cuts across the vertical lines at the top of the formal structure and functions as a coördinating, planning unit. At lower levels of the hierarchy, professional associations frequently perform a similar function of providing horizontal integration in a flat, loose formal structure.[4]

Above the superintendent in formal authority is a seven-member board of education, which sits concurrently as the board of education for the three different legal units that comprise the school system (elementary school district, high school district, and junior college district). In its own organization the board has eight permanent committees, with each board member serving on three or four committees.[5] This type of organization tends to bring the board members deep into administration. They have contact with several administrative levels below the superintendent; this situation makes the problem of professional-board relationships an acute one. In this report the board of education will be considered only where its policies shape adult education.

[4] The emergence of professional associations (e.g., associations of high school administrators, elementary teachers, etc.) and their relationship to the formal structure of state and local school systems would be a fruitful topic for sociological investigation. Particularly where organized on a state-wide basis, professional associations are major loci of political power within the educational hierarchy. The associations are, of course, relevant also to the problems of professionalization and standards maintenance.

[5] Budget and finance, building, cafeterias, insurance, law and rules, personnel and schools, purchasing and distribution, and transportation.

Adult education is under the jurisdiction of the Division of Extension and Higher Education. Within the division, adult education is now an important concern of both main branches—the junior college structure and the adult education branch. The focus of the next several chapters is upon the latter, which we have termed the "adult school organization."[9] The relationship of the junior college to the adult school is considered in chapter v.

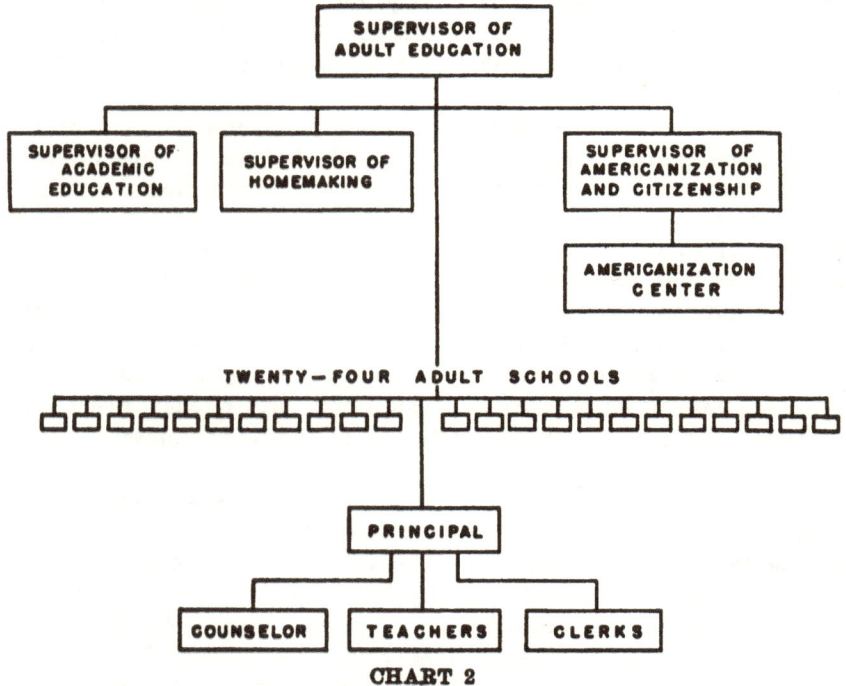

CHART 2

FORMAL STRUCTURE OF THE ADULT EDUCATION BRANCH, DIVISION OF EXTENSION AND HIGHER EDUCATION, LOS ANGELES SCHOOL SYSTEM, 1952–53

Diagrammed by the author. Several part-time supervisors (parent education, music) are not included.

The formal structure of the adult education branch is shown in chart 2. The supervisor of adult education (E. Manfred Evans) is the branch chief, responsible directly to the associate superintendent in charge of the division (Howard A. Campion). Line authority extends from Evans to twenty-four full-time adult-school principals. One supervisor (Amer-

---

[9] For a large urban school system, it seems useful to consider the entire system as an organizational complex composed of a number of subunits which in themselves constitute organizations.

icanization and citizenship) is also a line chief in charge of an Americanization center. The other full-time supervisors are in the headquarters office of the branch. Thus, in terms of discrete subunits, the branch is made up of the headquarters office, the Americanization center, and twenty-four adult schools located on senior high school grounds throughout the city.

The position of supervisor of adult education was established in 1936.[7] Evans, formerly an evening-school principal, was moved into this position at that time, and has since been the head administrator of the adult schools. Until the last five or six years, this administrative domain amounted to command over nearly all adult education in the Los Angeles schools. However, the supervisor does not have jurisdiction over the junior colleges, and with the considerable penetration of the junior colleges into adult education since 1948, large blocs of the program are no longer under his authority. The adult school program alone, however, is very large and well known, and Evans' position has given him state and national recognition.

The supervisory positions within the headquarters office are primarily staff positions within a line organization.[8] The supervisor of Americanization and citizenship is a staff adviser to the principals in this subject area, in addition to acting as principal of the Americanization center. The supervisor of homemaking is responsible for domestic science courses. The academic education supervisor is an administrative assistant to Evans, and this position has been used as a training post for prospective principals. Within the Division of Extension and Higher Education is a central office of business, trade, and apprenticeship supervisors whose operations are related to both the junior colleges and the adult schools. When dealing with the adult centers, their activities fall under the jurisdiction of the adult education branch.

In their formally constituted status, the twenty-four adult schools within this branch are now completely separated from high school administration. With their line of authority extending directly from a headquarters office, the principals are not under other field administrators. The principals are also the firing-line administrators of the program, as there are no important administrative levels beneath them.

---

[7] The present associate superintendent in charge of the Division of Extension and Higher Education moved into his headquarters position in 1934. When Evans was brought in two years later, all adult programs were placed under his jurisdiction. This involved bringing Americanization and citizenship into one administrative unit with the evening schools.

[8] The term "line" is used to denote executive positions in the adult schools, and "staff" to include the advisory curricular positions. The vocabulary of line and staff has recently been undergoing extensive criticism in public administration. See Simon, Smithburg, and Thompson, op. cit., chap. xiii.

In their school organization they have small clerical forces, teaching staffs, and from one to three counselors. Some counselors operate partly as vice-principals; the counselor position then provides a training post for potential administrators. Occasionally counselors are in charge of branch locations. The twenty-four schools have approximately three hundred branches, averaging about twelve per school. Branches are established at playgrounds, churches, hospitals, civic buildings, and business and industrial firms, as well as on elementary school grounds.

With twenty-four schools responsible to one headquarters office, the adult education branch has a lateral structure. This is not uncommon in large school systems; since each lower unit within a branch performs essentially the same kind of activity, the span of control of higher administrators is typically wide. This is apparent in the Los Angeles system in elementary, junior high, and senior high organization as well as in the adult education branch. Formally, this type of structure allows considerable autonomy to the lower administrators: the principals are geographically dispersed from headquarters, and the command structure is not densely populated with intermediary levels. The principals must be given some authority to administer the internal and external affairs of their schools. We shall later indicate, however, the ways in which their decisions are shaped by policies set at higher levels.

The principals and headquarter supervisors use their own professional group, the Los Angeles Evening School Principals' Association, as a coördinating instrument. Such associations tend to become a part of the formal structure, since permanent coördinating and integrating units are needed at various levels. The Principals' Association is quasi-formal: policy matters are sometimes referred to it by the board of education. Its recommendations represent a consensus among a large number of field administrators. This tends to give professional prestige to a policy stand and has tactical advantages in some situations. The association is also used for routine administrative matters.

The term "adult administrators," as used below, refers to principals of the adult schools, the branch chief, and, somewhat peripherally, the supervisor of Americanization and citizenship. These twenty-six positions may be considered the administrative posts of the adult school organization.

STUDENT CLIENTELE

We may now begin the examination of policies and procedures, taking first those that most directly relate to curriculum and clientele. The schools have common administrative procedures that determine the relationship between the adult organization and its students. Some rules stem from policies of the board of education; others are operating procedures that have arisen from practice, and have the approval of the majority of adult administrators.

SMALL-CLASS POLICY

Policy on small classes is of such importance to the school system that authority for its formulation is not delegated down the chain of command; it is set by top staff and the board of education. The establishing of a class-size minimum that governs both the introduction and the continuation of classes is one of the few areas of policy in adult education with which successive boards of education have concerned themselves. School records indicate the existence of a class minimum of fifteen as early as 1916.[9] This was changed to twelve in 1941-42,[10] and in 1952-53 was raised to fourteen.[11]

The budget division of the school system has had a strong hand in setting the minimums and checking upon compliance. To facilitate control by the board of education, the budget division must report twice a year (the second and seventh school months) to the board on the size of all classes. The reports for 1952-53 contained a breakdown, by school, of the number of classes under fourteen in enrollment, those from fourteen to twenty, and those with twenty or more, for a monthly average. The data in table 3 were adapted from one recent report. The adult schools had 1,719 classes operating during the second school month. In number of classes per school, the twenty-five schools ranged between 35 and 124, with an average of 68.8. Of the total number of classes, 3.7 per cent were under the policy minimum (this was after adjustments of the first school month), 37.4 per cent were between fourteen and twenty in attendance, making a total of 41.1 per cent with twenty or less. There was not much variation in attendance size between day and night classes (a breakdown not shown in the table): 410 classes, or 23.9 per cent, were given during the day, and of these, 44.1 per cent had twenty or under. Some 1,309, or 76.1 per cent, were evening classes, of which 40.1 per cent had twenty or under. "Twenty" is emphasized here, since classes below this level become a special administrative concern. Beginning enrollments are supposed to be clearly above this point; as classes slide down into the danger zone, special measures often need to be taken.

---

[9] Los Angeles School System, *Board of Education Files*, Minutes, March 20, 1916.
[10] *Ibid.*, August 7, 1941.
[11] "The class-size policy for 1952-53, as adopted by the Board on November 10, 1952, is a 'minimum for class continuation of 14 persons in average attendance per session over a one-month period.'" Communication to the Committee of the Whole from the Budget Division, no. 1, "Report on the Size of Adult Education Classes for the Second Month of 1952-53 from October 13, 1952, to November 7, 1952." Los Angeles School System, *Board of Education Files*, December 11, 1952.

TABLE 3

SIZE OF ADULT EDUCATION CLASSES BY SCHOOL, LOS ANGELES SCHOOL SYSTEM, SECOND SCHOOL MONTH, 1952–53

(Mean number of classes per school = 68.8)

Adult school	Number of classes by size of attendance			Total number of classes	Classes with 20 or fewer students (per cent)
	1–13.99 incl.	14–20.00 incl.	20.01 and over		
Banning................	..	46	20	66	69.7
Belmont................	9	34	36	79	54.4
Dorsey.................	3	18	34	55	38.2
Fairfax................	6	16	33	55	40.0
Francis Polytechnic....	2	28	45	75	40.0
Franklin...............	8	29	29	66	56.1
Fremont................	6	18	31	55	43.6
Garfield...............	4	20	19	43	55.8
Hollywood..............	1	32	91	124	26.6
Huntington Park........	..	33	39	72	45.8
Jefferson..............	1	23	34	58	41.4
Jordan.................	1	21	13	35	62.9
Lincoln................	9	21	32	62	48.4
Los Angeles............	1	32	82	115	28.7
Manual Arts............	1	25	50	76	34.2
North Hollywood........	..	24	53	77	31.2
Roosevelt..............	..	28	37	65	43.1
San Fernando...........	..	17	38	55	30.9
San Pedro..............	1	32	26	59	55.9
South Gate.............	..	18	38	56	32.1
University.............	..	40	46	86	46.5
Van Nuys...............	5	32	61	98	37.8
Venice.................	3	14	48	65	26.2
Washington.............	1	21	37	59	37.3
Americanization and Citizenship............	1	21	41	63	34.9
Total.............	63 (3.7%)	643 (37.4%)	1,013 (58.9%)	1,719 (100.0%)	41.1%

SOURCE: Adapted from official report, *Board of Education Files*, December 11, 1952.

Each class with fewer than fourteen students is listed in these reports by course title and average attendance. These are the classes requiring explanation, since each is a violation of the minimum requirement. By written and oral report the supervisor of adult education must explain to the board of education why these small classes have continued and what their disposition will be. In a separate memorandum, on the same day the foregoing report was submitted by the budget division, the adult education branch reported that 22 of the subminimal classes had been closed, 26 now had satisfactory attendance, 12 had been approved to continue, and 3 had their full cost paid by the federal government. A large number of unexplained violations would have been embarrassing for the professional administrators, from the principal on up to the superintendent, since the policy is a clearly stated board directive. Efficient compliance is an important index of the competency of the adult education branch administrators. Upon receipt of this budget memorandum, several board members wanted to know what was being done about the 63 small classes. An immediate reply to the board, in the form of a clearly stated report, was considered something of a victory by the adult administrators. Within a school system so large that third- and fourth-level administrators may be known to top management only in impersonal ways, an objective compliance with board directives is given special weight. Particularly for administrators of a marginal program, the mandates of board policy are not to be taken lightly. Implementation of the small-class policy is therefore a central concern of managing an adult school. The adult administrators do well for their own position when they cut away small classes with dispatch.

It is not difficult to perceive why the minimum-size requirement should be a core concern of board members and top professionals: it is directly related to a logic of economy in the administering of school programs,[13] and it is no accident that the budget division has been held responsible at times, if not continually, for ascertaining the proper minimum. The policy is an administrative response to the enrollment economy of adult education, with its close relationship between attendance, revenues, and local district costs. The small classes are deemed too great a burden upon local school funds.

Some of the ways in which this policy affects administration are apparent in the procedures of the adult school. Principals may initiate classes only where the immediate response from student groups is quantitatively good. Then, with the requirement that any class must be discontinued when a monthly average falls below fourteen, continuation depends upon the sustained interest of a dependable bloc of fifteen to twenty students, or upon a total enrollment large enough so that at least fourteen students appear at each session, or upon the replacement of lost students as the term progresses. In a program depending upon voluntary students, such a policy has a significant impact. Where students will not come, or after coming will not stay, that part of the program must be thrown out; the decision is made, not after a long period of trial and error, but immediately, in the first month in which enroll-

---

[13] For a discussion in a different context of cost and efficiency as management logics, see Roethlisberger and Dickson, *op. cit.*, chap. xxiv.

ment fails. In this way the policy narrows the discretion of line administrators in developing classes of limited appeal. Correlatively, the policy severely limits on-the-job training of teachers in new and difficult subject areas.

From table 3 it may be seen that six schools had five or more classes below the minimum in the second school month of 1952–53, *after* the weeding-out process of the first month. And six schools had more than 50 per cent of their classes in the under-twenty range. These data give some idea of the pressure that working against a minimum can exert on administration.

The alternatives in regard to small classes are to disband them, which involves dismissing teachers and sending away students; or to speed up the recruitment and turnout of students. Anticipation of these unpleasant alternatives warns principals against small classes. It is no exaggeration to say that the limits placed upon administrative choice by this one policy mean, in effect, that courses are selected *primarily* by class size. Occasionally, for the programs of greatest social responsibility, Americanization-citizenship classes and those needed for high school diplomas, it is easier to grant exemptions to the minimum. And where federal funds contribute to the support of a class, this also constitutes an extenuating circumstance (and evidence of the budget basis for the policy).

With these exceptions, the policy in regard to minimum class size is decisive in determining the schools' offerings. This is a clear example of the way in which a routine economy measure can intervene decisively in the content of a school program. The intervention, it must be emphasized, is not a peripheral matter. The professionals do not build a program while restricted merely by the limits of an annual budget. Rather, they work under specific directives to eliminate any subjects that are not immediately popular. Here it should be noted again that the minimum holds for all school months. Classes may collapse in December or in May, near the end of the term, as well as in the early weeks. As a consequence of this policy, determination of program content is largely removed from the discretion of line administrators and is given over to the objective criterion of student numbers.

Throughout the state, the enrollment economy is the basic determinant. It is under this condition, in combination with the others discussed in chapter ii, that boards of education and top administrators come to view class minimums as necessary. The small-class policy may be viewed as a basic response of central school administration to a set of historical conditions. The influence of these conditions is transmitted to the adult administrators from higher levels. For rational decision-making at the adult school level, the policy specifies a set of factual premises, and administrative behavior is shaped accordingly.

Since state funds for the program are not based on such units as a teacher hour, a class session, or a fixed annual apportionment, but on attendance, it is natural that the cost-attendance relationship will be taken into account by top administrators. And this relationship is most likely to loom large in their thinking when it concerns a program with an ill-defined, secondary position. If, in addition, program purpose is so open-ended that professionals are unsure about what ought to be done, the factual and judgmental premises for the policy are more clearly perceived. In a way, the policy hedges an uncertain situation by applying a logic of economy. With much confusion about what is a proper curriculum, the small-class policy simply determines that, whatever the content, it shall not cost too much (in terms of local taxes). The effect of the policy in ruling out certain types of programs seems unanticipated at the board of education level.

TUITION POLICY

A second policy area which receives attention from the board of education is tuition. The stand on tuition fees for adult students in the Los Angeles system is a firm no-fee policy, based primarily on arguments that adult administrators have been able to marshal in support of their interest.

The possibility of instituting tuition fees in the adult schools is periodically brought to the attention of board members by tax-minded interest groups: the California Taxpayers Association, the Chamber of Commerce, the Property Owners Association of California. These groups see tuition as a means of increasing income from the clientele of the schools and, at the same time, of curtailing the program. To take a recent example of tuition controversy, some adult classes of low repute were brought under fire during the preparation of the 1950–51 school budget. The tax groups suggested that fees be charged for these classes so that they could become partially self-sustaining. The board of education then sought a recommendation from the Los Angeles Evening School Principals' Association. The association advised against all tuition fees, as it had consistently in the past. In justification the administrators emphasized that tuition discriminates against low-income groups, and that the loss in state income from reduced enrollment on account of a fee would be greater than the tuition income.[13] The principals' recommendation was heeded and no fees were instituted.

[13] Recommendation of the Los Angeles Evening School Principals' Association, *Board of Education Files*, July 27, 1950.

Free tuition has been the policy in Los Angeles except during the year 1932–33. As that year was one of retrenchment in the school budget, it is difficult to assess the effect of a one-dollar fee upon the enrollment at that time. But for our purposes what really matters is the administrators' definition of the situation. In support of their position since that time, that tuition greatly reduces income from the state, the adult administrators point to the 1932–33 fee as a case in point. Regardless of the real cause for the decrease in average daily attendance, from 7,097 (1931–32) to 4,699 (1932–33), the decrease clearly represents a loss in attendance revenue much greater than the tuition gained, roughly $200,000 compared to $50,000. That fee decision was reversed within a year.

A tuition charge of any magnitude is considered detrimental by the program administrators. To the extent that favorable public sentiment is molded by participation in the adult schools—and the administrators believe this to be true—a narrowing of clientele diminishes public support and thus adversely affects organizational security. Where attendance is cut down, school income is reduced. A fee of $3 to $6, for example, as proposed by the economy interest groups, might threaten the very existence of the smaller adult schools. Such a fee could mean a cycle of smaller student bodies, cutbacks in organizational budget and personnel, and program restriction. These are possibilities that the adult administrators must take into account. And the threatened loss in state support constitutes a weighty premise in board decision-making for sustaining the principals' position. In the context of unpredictable results, but with a lower ratio of state support very probable, the logic of economy works *with* the administrators in convincing board members of the desirability of a no-fee policy.

This is not to say that moral issues play no part in such policy stands. Both professional administrators and board members need to consider the differential impact of fees upon high and low income groups. The relationship of adult education to the corpus of free public education also has to be considered. But even such moral issues usually have a practical aspect. The relationship of adult education to free public education, for example, ties directly to the position taken by the adult administrators in regard to tuition. The Los Angeles group seems especially anxious to avoid labels that would permanently set adult education aside from the main stream of public tax-supported programs. The principle of free education extends, in California, through grade fourteen. The adult administrators seek an extension of this concept to their student bodies. In contrast, tuition would separate the program from free public education, for the implication behind assessment is that the program ought to be partly self-sustaining from student fees. For those attempting to legitimize a central position for adult education within the school system, tuition is frequently considered to be a backward step. For the administrators defining tuition in this way, the cost-attendance relationship provides a lever for sustaining the no-fee policy.

It is clearly understood by administrators that tuition policy affects size of classes, types of courses, and the breadth of service to the community. Tuition acts directly upon student intent and commitment. As a barrier to loose entry into classes, it cuts down enrollment, especially the large attendance common in the first few weeks. Once paid, it tends to operate as an incentive for firmer ties to class and school. Where these effects are operative, tuition is an administrative mechanism for tightening student commitments.

The policy of no tuition means, on the other hand, greater student freedom. Students may sample courses at the beginning of a term, enter and leave classes at will, and drop courses readily. The no-tuition policy makes an important contribution to the operating procedures that have placed the students in a strategic position in the adult schools.

PROCEDURE FOR CLASS INITIATION

It is not feasible to introduce courses unless a certain level of popularity can be maintained. This determines an informally set policy that classes will not be instituted with fewer than twenty to twenty-five students, preferably more. Adult classes have a high attrition rate[14] and allowance must be made for it. In order to determine which courses are likely to survive, waiting lists are compiled for individual applications, and petitions are sent in by organized groups.[15] (For an example see Appendix V.) Both devices provide means by which interest can be signified by an

---

[14] The study of attendance problems has been a central topic of administrative research in adult education for a quarter of a century. Many references are contained in a review of the literature in Joseph W. Getsinger, "The History of Adult Education in the Public Schools of California," pp. 23, 28–31.

[15] For the five largest cities in California (over 120,000), Ferguson has shown that more than three-fourths of the adult classes in 1948–49 were recruited through these devices: 49 per cent of new classes had their origin in waiting lists, and 27 per cent in requests by organized groups. Philip M. Ferguson, "Practices in the Administration of Adult Education in the Public Schools of California," p. 88. In a presentation before the board of education on January 8, 1953, the Los Angeles adult administrators listed three means by which classes are commonly instituted: petition forms passed out to groups, the accumulation of individual requests, and advisory committees. Ferguson's data indicate that, as of 1948–49, advisory committees as a source accounted for about 5 per cent of the new classes.

aggregate large enough so that a course shows promise of survival. The idea for a particular course may have come originally from teachers, principals, staff, or outside individuals or groups. But in order to implement the idea, a large number of potential students must indicate some interest. This means that students or potential students make the decision whether the course will be instituted. Usually this is not a conscious decision, but it functions as the equivalent of a decision. Program building proceeds on this basis. Courses of general interest, or courses with a special public of their own, can be instituted.

What is emphasized here are the internal impulses for this basis of instituting classes. We need not have recourse to a vaguely formulated explanation attributing this type of course initiation to the demands of the people. Organizational dynamics must be understood. Where outside demands play an important role, we need to know what processes are involved, how such influences are transmitted, and why some organizations are more adaptive to certain types of demand than are others. In the adult schools, immediate pressures push administrative decision-making in this direction. There are concrete organizational reasons, stemming from the enrollment economy, why administrators base their decisions on the reaction of potential clientele. In this context we can understand why administrative memoranda on the introduction and continuation of courses are oriented toward the size-of-class problem. No other criteria approach this one in importance. When we realize that administrative behavior is constrained by the need for clientele, as mediated by small-class policy, we understand why this type of course initiation is necessary.

MODIFICATION OF CLASS AND TERM

Since class size is an important mandate upon administration, and the binding power of such devices as tuition fees is lacking, adult education has had to adapt to the exigencies of the student-school situation. Over the years there has developed the informal arrangement that students can enter and leave courses at any time. Usually, no home work is required and there are no examinations. Student obligations are difficult to enforce in the adult school environment, and frequently have the effect of reducing clientele; they have been virtually eliminated. With considerable attrition and turnover in most classes, and the teaching difficulties of sustaining interest over several months, there are manifold pressures upon administrators to shorten courses. The majority of classes in adult schools are still in the regular semester pattern, but the administrators have the authority to give courses of any length, and short courses are common. To take one example, in January and February of each year a number of the adult schools give courses, varying from three to eight weeks in length, in the preparation of income tax forms.[16]

The internal continuity of courses is modified also. Since students join at various times during a term and attend irregularly, there is a strong need for package classroom sessions. A package session is a discrete unit of information or practice having no necessary connection with previous sessions which students may have missed. Students are able to pick up or drop a course at any point, with minimal inconvenience. Perhaps the extreme example of the short course with package sessions is at the city jail, where the inmates, whose terms are comparatively brief, may attend classes. The supervisor of adult education has explained the special need for such sessions: "Each lesson is a unit in itself and as a person enrolls in that class he must go away with a complete unit of instruction. The instruction needs to be very carefully planned because of the turnover in those institutions. And so the question is not the length of the course, it is the length of the person in this particular instance."[17]

Many types of classes have been developed in which continuity of content has no relevance. Classes in sewing, upholstering, and radio and television repair involve working on materials brought from home. The students proceed at their own pace, and the teacher acts mainly as expert adviser. Sometimes he gives brief talks on technique, but these tend to be minimal where students are working at different speeds on various objects. In this type of course, standard devices for evaluating progress are not needed.

Another adaptation of internal course organization is the revolving-membership type of class. In the Los Angeles adult schools, driver education is conducted in this manner. The basic course consists of ten separate units of information and practice, not prerequisite to one another, given on ten different evenings. Students enter at any class session and go around the sequence until they come back to their own starting point. This constitutes course completion and the student can then take an examination which will serve as his written test, customarily given at the Department of Motor Vehicles, for a driver's license.

---

[16] These special occasional courses do not ordinarily appear in the schools' schedules of classes; they are advertised in newspapers and by printed announcements. This notice appeared in the Los Angeles *Daily News*, December 28, 1952: "Eight-week night school course in how to make out your income tax return will open January 8 at Washington Adult School, 10860 S. Denker Avenue."

[17] *Partial Report of the Senate Interim Committee on Adult Education*, 1953, p. 131.

Another common modification is the telescoping of a number of courses. In part this stems from the common practice of opening classes to all comers, with no entrance requirements. This means that members have a wide diversity of educational backgrounds, and beginning and advanced students crowd into the same classes. A teacher gave this example: "... in many adult-school classes in mathematics, one will find some studying simple arithmetic, others concerned with algebra or geometry, and yet others working on trigonometry or even calculus. Class demonstrations are useless; the teacher must move from small group or individual to individual."[18] This telescoping of courses is adaptive to the typical situation of student heterogeneity. Small blocs of students can be combined in order to keep classes above the minimum size.

Such informally derived procedures constitute policies set by the principals and frequently by the teachers themselves. They are answers to immediate problems of the work environment, with the enrollment economy the foremost factor. Again it must be emphasized that it is unrealistic to ignore the influence of this condition in constraining the behavior of administrators and teachers, especially since small-class policy translates a general condition of existence into a particular administrative mandate. These emerging norms, then, may be interpreted as functional for fulfilling the needs of the adult school organization.

The practice of initiating courses on the basis of their immediate appeal and of discontinuing those that lose popularity means that the program must, perforce, be composed of highly variable, unrelated parts. Two examples are given in Appendix VI, representing the largest and smallest schools of the adult education branch. The schedules are not complete listings, but represent the more stable offerings. However, they indicate the diversity of interest and content contained in a program, especially in the larger schools. And with courses initiated in an educationally *ad hoc* way (i.e., their entry into the program does not follow a predetermined scheme), there is little unity within the diversity. Integrating efforts of supervisors and principals can be sustained only within inherently narrow limits. The policies and procedures discussed above determine a *cafeteria-style program with considerable turnover of courses.*[19] Program fragmentation follows naturally from these procedures, while articulation does not.

---

[18] Respondent to teacher questionnaire. See Appendix II.
[19] Such terms as "considerable turnover" imply a comparative framework. "Considerable" compared to what? In each case the implied comparison is with regular high school and college programs.

EVALUATION STANDARD

In the adult school the assessment of course value becomes very difficult. Traditional methods of evaluation—written work, examinations, course accreditation—are not feasible, and there are no systematic techniques to take their place. Attendance has become *the* evaluational criterion, applied across the board to courses, teachers, and student groups. The adult administrators stress this as their basic standard.[20] Courses are deemed successful or unsuccessful on this basis, and it is felt that where students remain with a class they must be benefiting from it. The enrollment criterion is an objective, easily applied yardstick. Moreover, it reduces administrative anxiety by lessening the need for contending with purposes as criteria of course initiation and evaluation. With open-ended goals, purpose criteria have been ambiguous. The concreteness of the attendance criterion makes it highly serviceable in this context. The enrollment standard possesses an objectivity and universal meaning that is somewhat similar to the profit criterion of success in private business.

It should be understood that these operating procedures have arisen in the context of organizational marginality, with its pressures for adaptation. Until the marginality of the adult school is reduced, or special safeguards are given to the program, administrators must bank heavily on the survival and security potentialities of state aid. Thus marginality forces attention toward attendance. This condition holds for the adult education branch, though it has the largest public-school program in the country. The peripheral nature of the branch's present activity is partially indicated by its status as a 2 per cent item in the budget. Its direct expenses in 1952–53 were a little less than $2,500,000 in a school budget of approximately $118,000,000 or a little over 2 per cent.[21] The attendance contribution of the adult schools was 11,176 units out of 366,378 for the school system, or 3.05 per cent.[22] Table 4 indicates that program size, using average daily attendance as a comparative measure, has varied between 1.79 per cent and 3.89 per cent of the total system in the period 1925–26 to 1952–53. Comparing recent years with twenty-five years ago, the program has maintained about the same

---

[20] In a special meeting with the board of education in January, 1953, the Los Angeles adult administrators stressed that the chief instrument of curriculum evaluation is the "attendance that remains" in classes. Two other methods of evaluation were mentioned: reports by advisory committees and classroom visitation. It is realistic to stress, as the administrators emphasize, that the logic of the situation makes attendance the yardstick of evaluation. *Special Meeting of the Board of Education,* January 8, 1953 (field notes of author).

[21] Board of Education of the City of Los Angeles, *Controller's Annual Financial Report for the Fiscal Year Ending June 30, 1953.*

[22] *Ibid.*

TABLE 4
Relative Size of Adult Education by Average Daily Attendance, Los Angeles School System

School year	Adult education A.D.A.	Total high school A.D.A.	Adult education (per cent)	Total school system A.D.A.	Adult education (per cent)
1925–26	4,210	53,585	7.86	171,924	2.45
1926–27	4,938	62,070	7.95	183,460	2.69
1927–28	5,690	72,267	7.87	202,292	2.81
1928–29	6,133	75,506	8.12	206,444	2.97
1929–30	6,798	84,358	8.06	222,670	3.05
1930–31	6,980	90,591	7.70	231,701	3.01
1931–32	7,097	92,265	7.69	238,888	2.97
1932–33	4,699	94,871	4.95	243,685	1.93
1933–34	5,343	97,302	5.49	246,056	2.17
1934–35	5,613	99,205	5.66	246,516	2.28
1935–36	5,520	100,668	5.48	246,085	2.24
1936–37	5,404	105,540	5.12	250,925	2.15
1937–38	6,519	117,694	5.54	259,880	2.51
1938–39	6,876	121,560	5.66	259,442	2.65
1939–40	7,512	122,524	6.13	258,542	2.91
1940–41	8,592	120,944	7.10	253,479	3.39
1941–42	8,471	116,446	7.27	246,665	3.43
1942–43	5,116	104,140	4.91	235,182	2.18
1943–44	4,298	104,929	4.10	240,513	1.79
1944–45	4,983	107,986	4.61	249,317	2.00
1945–46	8,030	113,417	7.08	264,817	3.03
1946–47	9,451	122,885	7.69	300,196	3.15
1947–48	11,260	125,648	8.96	307,350	3.66
1948–49	12,304	129,346	9.51	320,329	3.84
1949–50	13,026	131,198	9.93	334,673	3.89
1950–51	11,882	127,004	9.36	333,844	3.56
1951–52	11,153	131,492	8.48	348,916	3.20
1952–53	11,176	136,581	8.18	366,378	3.05

Source: Board of Education of the City of Los Angeles, *Controller's Annual Financial Reports*. Percentages computed by author.

relative size. The adult schools have thus not become a larger segment percentage-wise, but have grown proportionately at a 2 to 3 per cent level with the over-all increase in an expanding system.

ORGANIZATION-CLIENTELE RELATIONSHIP

The foregoing policies and procedures mean that the adult school organization adapts to the currently expressed interests of the general population. The operating procedures determine the ways in which the adult school becomes highly sensitive to student demand, and develops what may be termed a *catering* relationship to its clientele. This evolution is not a result of the good or bad intentions of school personnel or of the personality of administrators, but a natural phenomenon of a social system. Under the circumstances, the normal response is the drift of programs toward the areas of largest student participation. For the undifferentiated adult population, these areas are mainly vocational training and avocational and recreational pursuits. The program drifts into these main channels and into others of good response. (See chap. iv on classes for organized groups.) And in order to maintain close contact with the changing foci of immediate interests, the administrators attempt to maintain the flexibility that will allow them to adapt readily. This type of adult program provides within education a unique kind of student-organization relationship. Nowhere else are students in a more dominant position. For teachers and principals the relationship to students is a job interest and an organizational mandate. They are constrained to encourage attendance. The students, on the other hand, may withdraw readily. Under these conditions the relationship of the adult school organization to its clientele approaches that of the customer-business relationship in which the customer is usually right.[23] The customer can come or go; the firm has everything staked on pleasing a sufficient number of customers. A similar relationship in the adult school context means that the lay side of the layman-educator relationship has a pervasive influence.

The quality of the relationship seems an extreme example of what is called, at other educational levels, the elective system. The study of college education during the first quarter of the century in this country suggests that an extreme elective system always provides a program intrinsically chaotic, with pronounced trends toward trivialization and a lowering of standards.[24] These are built-in tendencies wherever student choice plays the dominant role in course formation and maintenance. The adult administrators are, however, committed to this cafe-

[23] Veblen would have called it the intrusion of businesslike ideals into adult education. It is possible that the adult school relationship to students is an end point of a business-type adaptation in education. See Thorstein Veblen, *The Higher Learning in America*.
[24] Richard Hofstadter and C. DeWitt Hardy, *The Development and Scope of Higher Education in the United States*, pp. 53–54.

teria type of program. There is little program planning in the traditional sense of the term, and the drift of the program is relatively uncontrolled. The rise of the student body to a position of *dominance over professionals in influence on program content* is a central, defining characteristic of the adult school. A haphazard program development is a concomitant of this relationship between clientele and school, stemming from the tendencies of the organization to cater to the unstable popular interests of adults. This tendency may be viewed as a functional adaptation to organizational needs. (Chap. v suggests some dysfunctional aspects.) The development of the adult education branch, as for most departments in the state, is an adjustment to a mass market of interests and tastes—a market wherein the school has no guaranteed public.

THE TEACHING FORCE

There is one important position below the adult school principal in the organizational hierarchy, that of teacher. The formal structure of the adult education branch does not provide subadministrators such as vice-principals and department heads. The position of counselor has not yet assumed major importance. Here we need to examine some aspects of the teaching position and the composition of the teaching force. It may be assumed that the ways in which teachers are related to the school and to students are character-defining aspects of any educational agency. The purpose of this section is to assess the effects upon the teaching force of the policies that have most sharply defined it.

SELECTION AND EVALUATION

In the Los Angeles school system the authority for hiring adult teachers lies within the adult education branch. At the other school levels the selection process is centralized in the personnel division, which operates a formalized merit system that includes city-wide examinations, individual rankings, and selection by principals from approved lists. The administrators of the adult schools have been able to detach their teacher selection from these formal procedures. In the selection of personnel in the adult education branch, the personnel division has only a routine processing role.

The adult principals choose their teachers by means of informal interview, with the assistance of headquarters supervisors. Some supervisors have influence on teacher selection, but the actual choice rests with the field administrator. The initial selection is extremely informal. The principal has the authority to hire anyone he believes can succeed in the teaching post. No professional pre-job training is necessary, and applicants without credentials can readily be processed for an adult education credential. The procedure is simple and routine; certain types of credentials can be obtained from the State Department of Education upon the administrator's recommendation.²⁵ This leaves the principal free to select teachers on his own assessment of their competence and relieves the program of formal training requirements.

Why have adult administrators been given this special grant of authority? Because the informality of the selection procedure permits the principals to choose teachers who will be attractive to the different student groups, and to reject applicants who do not appear to fit the adult-class environment. A centralized, impersonal system would not permit this type of discretion. The informalizing of the selection process is a response to the organization's strong dependence upon a heterogeneous, loosely committed clientele. Since 1935 at least, the personal interview has been considered the one appropriate method of judging applicants.

> It is recognized by all workers in the field of adult education that personality characteristics are of fundamental importance for success in adult teaching. Such characteristics as poise, personal appearance, voice, a sense of humor, command of language, ability to meet people, and evidence of sincerity are more important in attracting and holding adult students than mastery of subject matter or philosophical background. The preliminary examination will, therefore, be one to discover these characteristics. The only method we know of for this purpose is the personal interview.²⁶

Evidently it has never proved feasible in the Los Angeles system to hire adult-school teachers on a civil service basis. The files of the school system indicate that, as far back as 1928, evening-school teachers were exempted from "competitive examination along civil service lines . . . required of all teachers and other applicants for educational positions in the Los Angeles City school system."²⁷

The current selection criteria of the principals are intuitive and unformulated. The appropriate personality type for adult classes is often described in such terms as "dynamic," "outgoing," "on his toes." In this very difficult matter of character assessment, the tendency is toward an extrovert stereotype. The inclination to use a personality formula is often reënforced by the administrator's limited knowledge of the subject matter in a broadly diversified program. To supplement his

---

²⁵ State regulations on adult education credentials are contained in *Administrative Code*, 1951, Title 5, secs. 381–403. The requirements specify alternative prerequisites (such as education or training) that make the credentialing of adult teachers flexible.

²⁶ Communication to the Committee of the Whole from the Service Division (Personnel Section), *Board of Education Files*, June 10, 1935.

²⁷ *Board of Education Files*, Minutes, December 10, 1928.

own expertise, the principal may obtain the counsel of high school principals in regard to teachers for academic subjects or he may consult outside experts for business and technical subjects.

On whatever basis it is done, the informal selection by principals is only the initial step that places teachers on the job. Once classes have begun, the students take over the selection process. Teachers, like courses, are tossed up in the program for student choice. It is the response of student groups to teachers as well as courses that determines in what direction the program will head.[28] The discontinuation of classes where the students have said "no" is the pragmatic device making the second and final selection. Mistakes made by the principal in his informal assessment are corrected as unsuccessful teachers are weeded out. In this way class size virtually takes over the selection of the teaching force.

This brings out an interesting comparison between the school system's formal selection of teachers at other levels and the nominally informal selection of adult education teachers. For, in place of the standardized procedure operated by the personnel division in typical merit-system fashion, there gradually arises an equally impersonal, standardized selection of teachers by the class-size requirement. This is *the* selection hurdle; in place of the competitive examination comes trial by enrollment. Further, this difference can be seen to have a special organizational meaning. In any large organization, some units operate as guardians of particular standards or aims. The personnel department is such a unit, creating and defending standards of employee selection and training. Although the field administrators of the adult school have been able to cut loose from this control, in an important sense it has not remained in the principals' hands but has slipped through to the classroom. The principals must obey student groups, instead of personnel standards, in teacher selection. The narrowing of administrative discretion by the demands of the enrollment economy has been the source of this switch of power from the personnel division to students. The adult administrators gain some survival potential for their organization in the process. Thus one important meaning of the enrollment economy in its impact upon the teaching force is that it has fostered the emergence of a *student-dominated selection system*. Selection criteria have shifted from professional preparation and competitive examination to judgment by student groups.

[28] MacKaye has emphasized this point. High-caliber teaching in one subject area will move the program in that direction. This fact can be used as an administrative stratagem in channeling program drift in desired directions. David L. MacKaye, "Problems Underlying the Administration of Adult Education in California," chap. v.

The importance of class size in determining the teaching force is realized by almost all teachers and administrators. One administrator devised an index of student holding power by which to evaluate his teachers. In this scheme an index score for each teacher was obtained by dividing the number of students remaining at the end of a course by the number beginning the course. Typically, however, the role of attendance in evaluation is not explicitly stated. It is simply understood by teachers that to remain in their positions it is necessary to comply with the board of education requirement on class size. Where classes do not initially measure up, a teacher may conclude that the time was not ripe or the subject matter was not appropriate. But once classes are under way, fading attendance brings the imputation that the teacher could not attract and hold adult students. Conferences with the principal on changing classroom techniques are then needed, and more effort must be put into getting out students. Failure in solving the enrollment problem constitutes failure in the teaching role.

In sum, an adult education organization with a diversified and highly changeable curriculum needs a flexible system of hiring and firing teachers. The teaching position must be brought into line with the basic requirement of program adaptability. For rank-and-file teachers, such a program means a hazardous employment situation. Especially where the teaching of narrow specialties is involved, the teaching position is highly vulnerable to arbitrary, sudden change. The teacher is linked closely to the specialty; for example, he may be a dental technician, a welder, or a landscape gardener. He must be dropped when student interest shifts, or a temporary demand is satisfied, or he becomes unpopular for any number of reasons. In the kind of organization that has emerged, the individual teacher must be dispensable.

Tenure and Turnover

It is clear that tenure and long-term security for teachers are not feasible within the adult school system. Too large a commitment of the teaching budget to tenured hours hampers administrative maneuverability in adjusting program and personnel. When for any reason the class enrollment of a tenured teacher shrinks below the allowable minimum, the teacher becomes an administrative burden. Funds that could be used for other more popular classes are tied down. Even more threatening to administration is the fact that shifts in student interest may cause a number of tenured teachers to become superfluous at one time. Moreover, any reduction in school budget places a principal's program in an inflexible position if a large share of the teaching funds is committed to a tenured staff. Faced with these conditions and possibilities, it has become operating procedure for the adult administrators to hold tenure to a minimum. There are provisions on the books for tenure and probationary status; these stem mainly from the state regulations for regular day teachers.[29] But it is the school system's policy that regulations for teacher permanency must give way in the adult program to more practical mandates.[30]

It is apparent that there is a real conflict between the interests of those in teaching positions and the administrative requirements of a

TABLE 5

TENURE STATUS OF ADULT EDUCATION TEACHERS, HIGH SCHOOL DISTRICT, LOS ANGELES SCHOOL SYSTEM, 1951–52

Tenured hours per week	Number of teachers	Percentage of all tenured teachers	Percentage of all adult education teachers[a]
4–9	28	14.5	2.8
10–14	67	34.7	6.6
15–19	52	27.0	5.1
20 and over (full time)	46	23.8	4.6
Total	193	100.0	19.1

[a] SOURCE: Personnel Division, Los Angeles School System. Based on 1,008 teachers on staff in January, 1952. These figures should be taken as approximations, since teachers move in and out of the program every month, and tenure records are not always complete.

flexible program. The control of permanent teacher status is a sensitive aspect of the principal's relationship to the teaching staff. Teachers interested in a career in adult education need to be convinced that a weak tenure status is one of the facts of life with which they must contend. Where teachers attempt to sit out their positions in the face of student attrition, administrative pressure for resignation must be applied. The conflict in regulations is sometimes solved by such informal devices as gentlemen's agreements, signed blank resignations, and voluntary leaves of absence until new classes open up. The administrators, however, prefer a legal solution to the problem, one that would make tenure regulations conform to the *de facto* situation, with permanent status contingent upon satisfactory performance in maintaining enrollment. The present tenure regulations are not considered feasible and, without administrative support, they are not viable.

A proximate picture of official tenure is available from school records. In adult education, teachers attain tenure for a specified number of

[29] State of California, *Education Code*, 1953, secs. 13081–13104.
[30] Los Angeles School System, *Board of Education Files*, Minutes, August 7, 1941.

hours per week; as seen in table 5, these ranged from four hours to twenty-five hours in Los Angeles in 1951–52. Teachers tenured by reason of their adult education position comprised about one-fifth of the total teaching force of the adult schools. Considering twenty hours a week the equivalent of a full-time teaching assignment, 4–5 per cent of the force had tenure at a full-time level. Teachers with tenure in other school programs cannot at the same time have tenure in adult education. In teaching time, these regular day teachers are limited to six hours per week in the adult program.

TABLE 6

INDICATION OF STAFF TURNOVER BY PERCENTAGE OF TEACHERS ON THREE YEARLY PAY LEVELS, ADULT EDUCATION TEACHERS, HIGH SCHOOL DISTRICT, LOS ANGELES SCHOOL SYSTEM

Location on pay scale	January, 1952		January, 1953	
	Number	Per cent	Number	Per cent
First year................	170	16.9	213	21.4
Second year...............	194	19.2	93	9.4
Third year or more........	644	63.9	688	69.2
Total................	1,008	100.0	994	100.0

SOURCE: Adult Education Branch, Los Angeles School System.

Since work in the adult school is a secondary job for most of the teachers, and the program is changeable in nature, there is considerable teacher turnover. Table 6 indicates that 17 per cent of the teaching force were new in 1952 and 21 per cent were in their first year in 1953. Between these two years, 213 teachers joined and at least 227 left the staff. This represents an understatement of turnover by a considerable margin, for these figures are based on January reports and do not include teachers who started in the fall of each year and then lost their jobs because of class terminations. In addition, the average turnover for individual adult schools would be higher than these overall percentages for the branch. The principals are able to shift some teachers from one school to another as they adjust their staffs to changing clientele requirements. The yearly turnover in teaching staffs ranges, at a minimum, between one-fifth and one-fourth.

The length of experience in adult education among the more successful teachers is indicated in table 7 ("successful" because they were still on the force in June). About one-fourth of the teachers (27 per cent) comprise a "hard core" that have been in service for ten years or more;

TABLE 7
DISTRIBUTION OF ADULT TEACHERS BY NUMBER OF YEARS TAUGHT IN ADULT EDUCATION

Number of years	Teachers	
	Number	Per cent
0–4	80	48.2
5–9	41	24.7
10–14	17	10.3
15–19	12	7.2
20 and over	16	9.6
Total	166	100.0

SOURCE: Mail questionnaire sample of teachers, June, 1953 (166 respondents to question 1).

TABLE 8
DISTRIBUTION OF ADULT TEACHERS BY YEARS OF SERVICE AND WORK HOURS PER WEEK

Number of hours	Years of service			Total
	0–4	5–9	10 years and more	
1–4	26	5	5	36
5–9	45	23	15	83
10–14	2	11	4	17
15–19	1	0	8	9
20 and over	1	1	10	12
Total	75	40	42	157

SOURCE: Data from mail questionnaire (157 respondents who answered questions 1 and 18). See Appendix II for text of questionnaire.

as shown in table 8, this group contains most of the teachers who teach a large number of hours. Eighteen out of twenty-one teachers working fifteen hours a week or more, in this sample population, are from this long-service group. None are day-school teachers. Two have occupations outside teaching, and sixteen are housewives or persons whose only employment is adult teaching. Fourteen of the eighteen are women. To work a large number of hours, they must teach during some daytime hours. The day classes are mostly domestic subjects, taught by women.

TABLE 9
Hours Employed per Week, Adult-School Teachers, Los Angeles School System

Number of hours	All teachers, January, 1953[a]		Questionnaire sample, June, 1953	
	Number	Per cent	Number	Per cent
1–4	273	27.5	40	23.4
5–9	482	48.5	88	51.5
10–14	94	9.5	17	9.9
15–19	64	6.4	10	5.8
20 and over	81[b]	8.1	16	9.4
Total	994	100.0	171[c]	100.0

[a] Source: Adult Education Branch, Los Angeles School System.
[b] Includes nine salaried Americanization teachers on regular high school schedule of thirty hours per week. All other adult-school teachers were on hourly wage.
[c] Total number of respondents answering question 18 of mail questionnaire.

TABLE 10
Occupational Types, Adult-School Teachers, Los Angeles School System

Occupational type	Teachers	
	Number	Per cent
Full-time adult teacher	16	9.4
Part-time adult teacher	155	90.6
Full-time day teacher	85	49.7
Full-time outside position	42	24.5
Part-time outside position	7	4.1
Housewife or no outside job	21	12.3
Total	171	100.0

Source: Data from mail questionnaire.

MULTIPLE WORK TIES

To the factors of student selection and weak tenure status must be added the multiple work ties of the teacher as a defining characteristic of the staff. Tables 9, 10, and 11 indicate some of the diversity in work hours and occupational ties. Using the January, 1953, figures in table 9, on hours employed per week, approximately 75 per cent of the teachers in the adult schools worked nine hours a week or less; 8 per cent had the equivalent of a full-time schedule. The last column in table 9 indicates that the mail questionnaire gives approximately the same percentages. Table 10 shows the diverse bases of the teaching

TABLE 11
PARTIAL LIST OF OUTSIDE OCCUPATIONS, ADULT EDUCATION TEACHERS, LOS ANGELES SCHOOL SYSTEM

Private industry	Public, religious, and medical agencies
Self-Employed	*Government*
Artist	Income tax examiner
Industrial relations consultant	Supervisor, Department of Motor Vehicles
Interior decorator	Teletype operator
Investment banker	
Public accountant	*Employed in Education*
Real estate appraiser	Clerk-typist, California State Department of Education
Aircraft Industry	Educational club director
Accountant	Interviewer, California State Department of Education
Draftsman	Payroll clerk, Los Angeles City Schools
Electronic instructor	Psychologist, Los Angeles City Schools
Electronic specialist	
Tool engineer	*Hospital*
	Educational therapist
Oil Industry	Mental hygiene director
Clerk	Personnel director
Welder	Personnel officer
Welding foreman	Physician (intern)
Building and Construction	*Church*
Electrical wireman	Church secretary
Engineering contractor	
Other	
Bank appraiser	
Buyer (instrument manuf.)	
Color consultant (interior decorating)	
Dental technician	
Retail meatcutter	
Sheet metal estimator	
Superintendent, importing firm	
Welder	

SOURCE: Data from mail questionnaire.

personnel, classified as full-time adult teachers, day-school teachers, those with outside employment, and housewives. The teachers who have positions outside teaching come from many occupations. Their occupational heterogeneity is indicated in table 11, which shows some of the outside jobs identified in the questionnaire data.

The most meaningful differentiation in sources of teaching personnel is between professional day-school teachers and lay teachers. As bases from which to recruit, each group has administrative advantages and disadvantages. Professional teachers have prior training in teaching techniques and are committed to the teaching vocation. But teaching interest is tied closely to their primary positions, with adult teaching as "more of the same" in the evenings. Day teachers often take on the additional evening work to supplement their incomes. As they improve their status on the regular salary schedule, they commonly expect to give up their evening work. There is sentiment within administrative ranks that the day teachers, who deal with adolescents, are incapable of handling adults; they are too theoretical. The corollary belief is that lay teachers are more appropriate. From outside sources it is possible to obtain experts in a wide range of specialties who are interested in part-time teaching as a fundamentally different kind of work from their ordinary occupations. However, they are likely to be lacking in teacher training and experience.

As a long-run trend over the last twenty-five years, there has been more recruiting from outside sources and less from day-teacher ranks.[51] In the 1920's, night teaching was almost completely preëmpted by day teachers. This is not true today, and least so in urban centers. The important point, however, is that administrators have the authority to shift the recruiting base of the teaching force according to program adjustments and staff tenure. The advantage of using people already employed in the school system is that they cannot claim permanent status in the adult program. Utilizing a large number of day teachers three to six hours a week keeps a program maximally flexible. Thus one way to ease tenure pressures on the teaching budget is to move the personnel base back toward day-school teachers. The social base of the teaching personnel is also somewhat affected by program content, with academic components usually drawing upon professionally trained teachers. But this is not always true. Classes in English and history may be taught by outsiders, since classes even in traditional areas tend to become specialized and practical in adult education: English courses become "Short Story Writing," and "Radio-Television Script-Writing." The more specialized the courses, the more likely that outside experts will be found.

---

[51] The head of the Bureau of Adult Education has expressed this belief: "The trend in adult education is definitely in the direction of employing more teachers with practical background and fewer teachers with a purely academic background." *California Schools*, 22, no. 11 (November, 1951), p. 400. Ferguson has shown this to be true for the period 1930–1948. Ferguson, *op. cit.*, p. 91.

These characteristics of the instructional staff indicate some of the ways in which the enrollment economy shapes the teaching position. Teachers are selected and evaluated by their students; tenure and job security are weakly established; and most teachers have other primary occupations. These are core aspects of a teaching staff built under the mandates of the enrollment economy and the marginal position of the adult schools. A full-time, tenured staff with adult teaching as primary vocation is *not* functional for the survival and security of the organization. For the administrators to protect the organization and program with which they are identified, they must allow the teaching force to be shaped in these ways.

The part-time, dispensable type of teacher is symptomatic of the latent force of organizational needs. When we perceive the burden that a rapidly changing, part-time staff places upon administrators, and, at the same time, review the perennial conferences and pronouncements on the importance of a professional staff, we realize the strong and conflicting pressures to which they are subjected. The maintenance of organizations must take precedence over desires for a trained, full-time, well-committed staff. This trend develops in spite of warnings by many that the quality of the staff is dependent upon full-time employment and permanent tenure. Morse A. Cartwright, a national adult education spokesman, asserted twenty years ago, "Real strides in quality of teaching will not be made until men and women are undertaking careers in adult teaching on a full-time basis, undisturbed by other vocational interests."[32] Some superintendents in California have expressed a similar belief.[33] Adult education workshops report that "interests of adult education teachers [are] not primarily in the profession since most of them are only part-time adult teachers," and recommend as a possible solution "a corps of full-time adult education teachers."[34] Within the Los Angeles system the problem of making adult education a profession has frequently been posed. No realistic solution has been forthcoming. Operating pressures have not permitted the development of an autonomous teaching force.

PROFESSIONALISM

The needs of the organization have thus made it mandatory that teach-

---

[32] Morse A. Cartwright, *Ten Years of Adult Education*, p. 184.
[33] Will C. Crawford (Superintendent, San Diego School System), "Purposes and Personnel Administration of Adult Education," *passim*, esp. pp. 469–471.
[34] State of California, Department of Education, Bureau of Adult Education, *Report and Proceedings of the Montecito Workshop in Adult Education*, 1952, p. 101.

ing shall in the main be nonprofessional. The following characteristics of the work force are indicative of this status:[*]

1. *A weak tenure-seniority system.* Continuity of employment is dependent upon student reaction and program drift. Therefore, length of service is no protection against arbitrary termination of employment.

2. *A weak career pattern.* A teacher cannot predict an ordered career leading through several stages of rank and pay. The maximum amount of progress is determined by a three-step pay scale, based on the first, second, and third years of service. A weak career pattern results from lack of tenure and stabilized working conditions.

3. *Remuneration by wage rate.* Salary tends to be a mark of professionalism in various fields, with the work commitment not measured by the hour. There are several reasons why the wage-salary difference is especially important in adult education. First, all other levels of teaching are salaried. Second, in the attempts of teacher groups to raise the status of their occupation, the importance of annual salary as a professional characteristic is repeatedly emphasized. The California Teachers Association stresses the job attributes and attitudes of the professional worker, who does not work by the hour and does not expect to be paid on that basis.[*] The criteria of the C.T.A. are factors which by the nature of the position are not characteristic of adult teaching.

4. *Lack of entrance standards.* Training is restricted mainly to what is acquired after entry into the job. Distinctive preparatory training, however, usually provides a differentiation between professional and nonprofessional status: a set pattern of preparation is essential for entry into a profession.

5. *Little opportunity for professional norms to emerge.* It is through common preparatory training, long-term work commitment, and sense of community that professionals come to establish their own rules of conduct. The structure of the adult-school teaching position militates against an emergent teacher community that would control the behavior of its members.

These characteristics of a weakly professionalized staff are not easily changed in the adult school, for the system is resistant. Under the conditions of organizational existence, teacher incentives must shift from long-run professional guaranties of secure employment and distinctive

---
[*] This discussion utilizes some categories suggested by Foote in an analysis of professionalism in another context. See Nelson N. Foote, "The Professionalization of Labor in Detroit," *American Journal of Sociology*, 58, no. 4 (January, 1953), pp. 371–380.

[*] "Code of the Professional Worker," *CTA Journal*, 49 (April, 1953), p. 15.

status to short-run incentives such as the hourly wage rate. This is the main reward that the organization is able to offer in return for the time and energy of its rank-and-file teachers.

IDENTIFICATION WITH ADULT SCHOOL

The commitment of teachers to the adult school has been discussed thus far in terms of objective characteristics of the teaching force. From the questionnaire mailed to teachers, information was gathered on the teachers' identification with the adult school. Question 7 of the questionnaire pertained to the identification of teachers with what has now become a central purpose of the administrators—the diversification of the program. How do the teachers feel about further widening of program content? The response was as follows:

	Number	Per cent
(1) The program should have a *greater* variety of courses	48	27.3
(2) The program should remain about as varied *as it is now*	114	64.8
(3) The program should have *less* variety of courses	14	7.9
Total	176	100.0

The majority of the teachers upheld the present dimensions; thus identification with purpose may be said to exist to a fair degree.

A second aspect of identification lies in teachers' identification with one another. It is assumed that meaningful identification with an organization involves not only some agreement with its purposes but identification with other personnel. Questions 8–11 were concerned with this dimension.

	Number	Per cent
8. What is the nature of your contact with other adult-school teachers?		
(1) I am *very close* to other adult-school teachers	15	8.6
(2) I have *some contact* with the other teachers	98	56.0
(3) I have *little or no contact* with the other teachers	62	35.4
Total	175	100.0
9. Are you concerned with the opinion in which you are held by the other adult-school teachers?		
(1) I consider their opinion *quite important*	67	38.3
(2) I am *mildly concerned* about their opinion	60	34.3
(3) I have *little or no concern* about their opinion	48	27.4
Total	175	100.0
10. During the past year, have you discussed the content of the adult education program with other adult-school teachers?		
(1) I have discussed it *numerous times* with other teachers	34	19.4

	Number	Per cent
(2) I have discussed it *a few times* with other teachers..........	95	54.3
(3) I have *not discussed* it with the other teachers.............	46	26.3
Total................	175	100.0
11. Is it important to you whether or not the adult-school teachers spend more time together than they do now?		
(1) I consider it *quite important*.............................	33	18.9
(2) I consider it to be of *some importance*....................	88	50.3
(3) I consider it of *little or no importance*....................	54	30.8
Total................	175	100.0

Questions 8 and 10 concern the teacher's closeness of contact with other teachers and discussion of program content with them; question 9, the opinion of one's peers; question 11, the teacher's attitude toward involvement. These four items are related to identification with the teaching force; the "identified" person tends to give positive answers, and the "nonidentified" to give negative answers.

The answers to question 8 indicate that few respondents feel in close contact with other teachers. They rarely see one another and know few of the other teachers, since their part-time employment is scattered over different days of the week, different hours of the day, and different plant locations. Thus neither formal nor informal contacts are frequent, and close association is not likely to emerge.

Question 9 reveals the most positive pattern of response, with over a third of the teachers considering the opinions of other teachers important. This was unexpected, and is out of line with the pattern of response to the other three questions. Obviously, the sixty-seven teachers who feel that the opinions of other teachers are "quite important" do not, at the same time, assess their present relationship as very close (question 8) or consider it important that closer relationship be established (question 11). Individual status in the eyes of others, even when not close to them, may have intruded here; the pattern does seem to indicate a concern with the judgment of one's peers.

Question 10 on discussion of program content with other teachers should have special indicative power, since it was answered at the end of two years of public controversy over what the adult school ought to be doing. The four-month period preceding June, 1953, was one of especially sharp attack and defense; the principals worked intensively to mobilize support from the teachers and the public. Question 10 would indicate that the nature of the teaching position did not permit great involvement here. In a year of controversy, a large number of

TABLE 12

TEACHER IDENTIFICATION, BY OCCUPATIONAL SOURCE

Identification score[a]	Day-school teacher		Person with outside job		Adult teaching only[b]		Counselors[c]		Total	
	Number	Per cent	Number	Per cent	Number	Per cent	Number	Per cent	Number	Per cent
High (4–6)	11	12.9	9	20.5	10	26.3	5	71.4	35	20.1
Medium (7–9)	43	50.6	17	38.6	21	55.3	2	28.6	83	47.7
Low (10–12)	31	36.5	18	40.9	7	18.4	0	0.0	56	32.2
Total	85	100.0	44	100.0	38	100.0	7	100.0	174	100.0
Mean[d]		8.8		8.4		7.6		5.9		8.4

[a] Combined score for questions 8, 9, 10, and 11 of mail questionnaire. A score of 4 represents high identification; 12, low identification.
[b] Includes full-time teachers, part-time teachers with no other work, and housewives.
[c] This column does not refer to occupational base as do the other columns, but the counselors have been segregated here to show their greater degree of identification. Five of the six counselors appearing in this questionnaire sample were day-school teachers; one had a full-time position outside the school system.
[d] Computed from ungrouped data.

teachers had not discussed the program with their peers. The pattern of response is in harmony with that of question 8.

The last of these four questions relates to the need for greater participation. Here again the answers lean toward the negative side. As several respondents said in appended comments, there was no reason, in their highly specialized, part-time positions, to get together with other teachers. The basis of common interest is narrow. Thus more time with other teachers is costly to the individual in the sense of requiring free time after working hours. The effort of the administrators to foster teacher identification and participation is an uphill pull in this context, working against unfavorable social conditions.

In order to study the impact of occupational sources upon the identification of teacher with teacher, the answers of each person to the four questions were combined in a composite score. The total scores, using values of one, two, and three for the answers to each question, range from four to twelve; four is well identified and twelve is low identification. The distributions of scores within teacher groups classified according to occupational bases are given in table 12. With considerable heterogeneity within each category, no clearcut differences appear between the major occupational types. From these data, predictions could be made only at the extremes: counselors tend to score toward the well-identified pole, and day-school teachers are rarely at this extreme. The column means indicate, however, that, when these categories are defined as bases of the work force, identification increases as we proceed from the day-school source to the community basis to the adult teacher.

The identification of teachers with each other is a fundamental aspect of identification with the organization. Organizational symbols become meaningfully related to individual members when they are mediated and supported by other participants through small group ties within the teaching staff. The identification of teacher with teacher in the adult school is likely to be weak because the conditions for the establishment of small social groups are weak. It is difficult for teachers to feel a sense of community in this unusual environment.

An attempt was made in the questionnaire to gather information on teacher identification with certain program practices. Here attention was centered on the procedure of adding classes according to demand, and the specific policy of discontinuing classes when they fall below a stated minimum. A question was asked about school standards also.

12. From your experience, would you say that the adult schools
have definite teaching standards?

	Number	Per cent
(1) The adult schools have *definite* teaching standards..........	116	67.0
(2) The adult schools have *vague* teaching standards...........	52	30.1
(3) The adult schools have *no* discernible teaching standards....	5	2.9
Total.................	173	100.0

Here the teachers defend the adult school as having a platform of standards. This was contrary to expectation, since the operation of a changeable, diversified program involves vaguely formulated norms of teacher conduct. Later interviews concerning this item revealed that the yardstick of small-class policy was itself considered a standard. The ambiguity in this question was not caught in pre-testing.

The three questions relating to identification with operating norms are as follows:

13. Do you feel that, in general, courses should be *added* to the program according to the demand for them?

	Number	Per cent
(1) Courses should *always* be added according to demand.......	84	50.0
(2) Courses should *sometimes* be added according to demand.....	84	50.0
(3) Courses should *not* be added according to demand..........	0	0.0
Total.................	168	100.0

14. Do you feel that a teacher should be dismissed when his classes fall below a certain minimum size?

(1) I feel that the teacher *should be dismissed*.................	32	19.1
(2) I feel that other factors should be considered and the teacher *frequently kept on*..........................	123	73.2
(3) I feel that class size should not be important, and the teacher *definitely kept on*...........................	13	7.7
Total.................	168	100.0

15. In your opinion, does the policy of discontinuing small classes have a beneficial or a harmful effect on teaching?

(1) It has a *beneficial* effect................................	44	26.2
(2) It doesn't have much effect either way....................	42	25.0
(3) It has a *harmful* effect.................................	82	48.8
Total.................	168	100.0

In the pattern of answers, valuations noticeably shift from positive to negative according to three different aspects of demand-attendance procedures and their impact on the teaching position.

In question 13 the consensus is that student requests should play an important role in adding courses to the program. No one took the position that demand was not a relevant criterion, and 50 per cent responded that courses should *always* be added according to demand. Thus teachers seem identified with demand doctrine as it relates to the bases for initiating classes and teaching jobs.

Question 14 concerns the relationship between demand and the continuation of classes: when demand falls off, classes should be disbanded. Here an interest in job maintenance undoubtedly enters, and the consensus shifts toward advocating criteria other than just class size when considering the dismissal of teachers; three out of four maintain that the teacher should frequently be kept on when his classes fall below a stated minimum. In written and verbal comment about this question, teachers pointed out that there are extenuating circumstances, that it is not always the teacher's fault.

In question 15 the pattern of answers is negative. One out of four maintain that discontinuing small classes has a beneficial effect; two out of four say it harms teaching. It should be remembered also that the teachers answering these questions were the successful ones—still on the force in the last school month of 1953. Those weeded out between September and June because of low attendance undoubtedly would have stressed the harmful effects of this policy. The main point, however, is that the question presents a situation faced by most teachers at some time, whether they are successful or unsuccessful: time and energy must be given to the work of maintaining classes (e.g., telephone solicitation of recalcitrant students), and courses must be adapted to meet this basic need.

Thus there is no uniform, logically consistent identification of teachers with the demand-attendance procedures of the adult school. They approve or disapprove according to the way in which the teaching position is affected. They tend to approve demand as the basis for introducing courses, to disapprove it as the basis for discontinuing classes, and to dislike its impact on teaching.

Social Structure

The materials presented thus far in this chapter permit a few summary statements on the sociological nature of teacher participation in the adult school. The teaching level is characterized by a weak social structure. First, there is little informal contact between teachers. The weakness of group ties stems directly from the nature of the teaching position as a technical job of limited commitment. Compared to day-school teaching, there are no common duties, no common lunch periods, frequently no common hours and days of work, and little mutuality of interest. Thus it is no accident that a closely knit group structure among teachers is found in very few adult schools. Principals define the situation as unfavorable, as a problem. They state that teachers come to the main office only to get their room keys, arrive five minutes before class, and depart immediately afterward. Some principals provide a staff room and such inducements to informal participation as coffee snacks, and are not surprised when they get little or no response.

Second, there is little informal leadership within the ranks of teachers. Without an interlocking structure of group ties, there is little opportunity for leadership to develop informally. For example, few teachers want to become active in the adult education associations available to them.[57] To represent a school on the executive council of an association is regarded as a duty rather than an opportunity. There are few volunteers, and the principal must prevail upon someone to fill the post. Leaders in these organizations, when asked why teacher participation is so inadequate, suggest that neither the regular day teacher nor the person from an outside occupation has any real reason for active commitment. Those who are interested in strengthening the associations and in defending adult education seem to be those whose only teaching is their adult-school post and who at the same time want very much to hold on to their jobs. This would seem the durable basis for involvement and a sense of commitment and thus for the creation of active groups from which leadership will spring.

How, then, does the social structure of this work force compare with that found in other contexts? Compared with industrial workers, the rank-and-file members of the adult school operate on a highly individualistic basis, even more than regular public-school teachers do. They perform specialized tasks in separate rooms, in close contact with "customers" but out of contact with other employees. The individual teacher does not have to take into account other teachers' reactions to what he does. Few know or care about his work, and informal social controls are not available.

Ordinarily, work codes are upheld by professional identification and an informally derived social structure. The individual participant is linked to other workers by mutual interests, social ties, and a professional or semiprofessional commitment. This usually holds true for teachers, architects, social workers, chemists, engineers, and numerous other groups. But in the adult school both professionalism and informal social structure are lacking. There are no common definitions in a teacher community of proper teacher behavior, and there is little op-

---

[57] The Adult Education Association of Los Angeles and the southern section of the California Council of Adult Education.

portunity for a tradition to emerge in the form of written and unwritten codes transmitted and enforced by peer groups. A weak social structure means that work codes among teachers will be weak, for social ties are the real bulwarks of norms and values.

Where inter-teacher ties are lacking because of the basic nature of a work position, we find a tendency toward the individuated technician who is cut loose from peer-group controls and free to adapt to those who really count in the situation—the students. This tendency has fateful consequences for the educational process. It evidences diminished strength of teachers as a work force and an increase in the power of students and administrators. Informal control of teacher behavior by peers, which plays an important role in full-time, integrated teaching staffs, gives way to control by students and the formal rules of administration. The most notable feature of this change is the tendency toward student dominance.

THE ADMINISTRATORS

The typically weak commitment of teaching personnel to an adult school organization reduces their part in activities related to the total enterprise, such as defending the program against attacks, working for the welfare of the organization, and maintaining standards over the long run. The burden of such concerns falls upon the shoulders of the small group of principals and headquarters supervisors. They provide core continuity in the organization, and have more influence in determining the ultimate character of the adult school than they would have if the teaching staff were a stable, professional group. Thus the administrative role is very important.

ADMINISTRATIVE AUTHORITY

Previous discussions in this chapter have suggested the tenor of administrative thought and action, and hence the analysis will be of a summary nature here. There is considerable decentralization of authority from headquarters to field units in the Los Angeles organization. The geographic dispersion of schools provides a natural basis for administrative autonomy; this tendency toward field authority is reenforced by the horizontal structure of the adult education branch.

In spite of formal decentralization, however, the principals' authority is restricted in several ways—for one, by the small-class policy. In addition to this type of fixed limitation on authority, there are others that shift with the pressures of the day. Program building is usually limited by considerations of general organizational welfare. "Dangerous" courses are avoided. The threat to the total organization at any particular time depends on the channels of interest into which segments of the program are moving and the pressure of interest group representatives, state legislators, and administrators of the other school levels. The definition of "dangerous" is set by the intensity of the threat, real or anticipated, posed by critics. Large forums become dangerous at one time, square-dancing at another, and lampshade-making at a third. When, for any reason, the attention of outsiders is focused on some of the schools' sensitive courses, then the welfare of the entire adult education branch is involved—indeed, as is that of the entire school system. Controversial courses tend to come under the strict control of headquarters. Venturing into "hot" program areas requires special clearance. One effect of the controversy which eddies around the program is to reduce the authority of field administrators. When criticism is severe, coördination must be tightened to ensure against moves rendering the entire organization vulnerable. Limits on the principals' decision-making tend to expand or contract according to the ebb and flow of controversy.

Thus the administrative authority of adult administrators in program building is bound in by class size requirements and the pressure that critics can bring to bear. The principals are necessarily concerned also with attendance because of its basic import for the operating budget and the maintenance of administrative positions. But within these limitations they are free to build their own staffs (as affected by student selection) and to introduce courses in which they are interested. Some principals attempt to give preference to the well-accepted, traditional subjects that lead to a high school diploma. At the same time, the open-endedness of program purpose permits the principals to experiment with whatever will be successful in attracting students, as long as counterpressures are not too strong, and to institute courses that will strengthen their position with the community.

Administrative Orientation

Marginality, diffuse goals, and the pressures of the enrollment economy lay the basis for a strong "other-directed"[20] orientation on the part of

---

[20] Riesman uses this concept to denote the type of character of many persons in modern society. "Other-directed" behavior is especially sensitive to outside cues from the immediate environment, in contrast with inner-directed and tradition-directed behavior. Of special interest here is that other-directed behavior can be the product of role mandates as over against the dictates of personality. In the present context the term is used to refer to the orientation of a work role. Personal experience with administrators indicates a range of personality types among them, with many tending to be inner-directed men. The pressure of the job, however, is to force other-directedness regardless of character type. See David Riesman, *The Lonely Crowd*.

adult education administrators. They tend to face outward, toward clientele and critics, not inward toward traditional rules and their own conception of right and wrong. The pressures of the enrollment economy foster sensitivity to outside demands; insecurity resulting from marginality reënforces this sensitivity, and open-ended purpose encourages it.

The importance of the other-directed orientation is evidenced by the administrative duties that are deemed most significant. Administrative duties may be divided into three categories: routine school administration; selection, training, and supervision of teachers; and community relations. Overriding the internal duties in importance is the work outside the schools. Some of this emphasis appears in the following description by the supervisor of adult education:

In Los Angeles we like to have Principals organize and direct the program in the various communities. We want the Principal to be one who has extensive community contacts. We want him to be enthusiastic; to be a promoter; to be an evaluator; to be one who is alert to organize and develop any proper educational program, in any place at any time, which will serve the adult community in which his school is located.[20]

The principals are expected to build programs that will service a particular neighborhood. They are to canvass individual and group desires by means of the petition, the sign-up list, and informal assessment. They are expected to take an active part in community voluntary associations; a good adult administrator is effective on the "luncheon circuit." This type of work not only results in a larger number of classes but has value in improving public relations. Also, to protect themselves against program restrictions by higher authorities, the principals give attention to political activity. This was evident in 1952–53, both in relation to the state legislature, which was considering restrictive legislation, and the local board of education, which was dubious about the value of many courses. For a number of reasons, then, the role of the administrator becomes that of a salesman-promoter, and the adult administrator often speaks of himself in such terms.

In this way the highly competent "modern" principal becomes defined as one who is vocal in championing adult education, and adroit in developing community contacts. As a concomitant, internal administration and the training of a teaching force tend to be deëmphasized. Supervision, in particular, becomes devalued as a proper activity of the administrator. Some of the more conservative of the Los Angeles

---

[20] E. Manfred Evans, "Adult Education in Los Angeles City Schools, 1948–49," *New Los Angeles School Journal*, 32, no. 3 (October 18, 1948).

principals note that those new in the ranks tend to take the promoter type of administrator as their model. The "educator" role is played down. Little emphasis is placed upon academic background in the selection of principals, since the need is pressing for a community-relations man. The incumbent must be able to adjust to manifold types of requests, organize appropriate classes, and acquire competent teachers. It would not be unfair to characterize the administrator as a broker between outside requests and a supply of courses and teachers which he arranges to fit the demand.

Social Structure

Social support among principals is much stronger than it is among teachers. In part this stems from the fact that there are few principals, and they share the same problems. Permanently committed to the program, they have a feeling of responsibility toward it. Attacks upon the program over a long period of time have caused them to draw together in common defense and mutual support. Moreover, their conditions of work favor the development of close relationships and strong sentiments. There is much joint committee activity and more face-to-face interaction than would be supposed, in view of the fact that administrators are spatially separated in the various schools.

Another factor is that the adult administrators have common feelings of isolation from the rest of the school system. This is supported by the results of an inquiry made in the Los Angeles school system in March, 1953, by the Science Research Associates. Their investigation was concerned with attitudes and opinions throughout the school system.

> The [adult administrator] group seems to feel rather removed from the main channels of the education program, and apparently suffers from defeatism and pessimism, as demonstrated by a number of different items. Almost one-half of this group feels that there would be more opportunity for advancement in another place. They do not gain as strong a sense of "belonging" as other groups, even though they may work in the system for years. ... A relatively large number would not choose teaching as their profession, were they to start over again. ... They feel that they get too little attention from the administration, and that too many decisions are made without their consultation. ... All of these items suggest that there is some unrest and insecurity felt by the principals in adult education.[40]

The Associates noted that, at the same time, the principals had a relatively strong *esprit de corps* and confidence in the adult education movement. The in-group sentiment is probably bolstered by the feeling of alienation from central school administration.

[40] From the summary of major findings in a survey by Science Research Associates, Inc., *Attitudes and Opinions of Educators: The Los Angeles City School System*, March, 1953.

The sentiment among administrators in support of the program and one another is so strong that at times it becomes fanatical. A long history of controversy has fostered the tendency to strike back vigorously at program critics with a strong defense of all administrative behavior. Epecially when the principals are under pressure from the state legislature, it constitutes treason for any of them to voice misgivings about the school program. Departure from a straight-down-the-line defense is construed as giving aid and comfort to the "enemy." The sense of belonging to an educational movement of the future, one that must be sustained at all costs, supports the administrative group in times of crisis and provides much of the cement for group solidarity.

Thus a basic differentiation between the administrative and teaching levels of the adult school organization in Los Angeles is the nature of the social structure and the strength of group feeling. Relationships among the teachers tend to be segmental and impersonal; the adult school is likely to be seen as expendable, since the teachers are not identified with the school as a permanent source of psychological satisfaction and group feeling. The administrators, on the other hand, have core participation in the sense of being key organizational agents and also in the sense of interaction within a peer group. They become attached to their schools as unique sources of personal satisfaction, and usually define themselves as permanent, important members of an educational movement.

CHAPTER IV

SERVICE AND LEGITIMACY

THE previous chapter has indicated the service orientation of adult-school administrators in searching out consumer preferences and adapting programs to these desires. The adaptation is not merely programmatic, however: the relationship between student and school is altered, the teaching staff is modified, and administrative energy is channeled into external duties. A fundamentally different type of educational agency emerges, a type that may be termed a service organization. This refers to a kind of school that caters directly to consumer desires. It is important to distinguish this meaning of service from "service" as a public relations slogan.

Educational administrators at all levels present their programs as a service to the community. The service terminology is now an important part of the public relations doctrines that have developed within education. A recent declaration of the point of view of the Los Angeles school system begins with the summary statement: "The Los Angeles City Schools serve people of all ages, abilities, interests, races, creeds, national and socio-economic backgrounds."[1] Such statements are intended to be good public relations and also to benefit employee morale. When such statements are *merely* organizational slogans, they tell us little about core aspects of organizational behavior. In the adult school context, however, verbalisms about service are indices of a basic orientation. Service slogans thus take on a deeper meaning, becoming an expression of a distinctive type of school. The idea of service conceptualizes a real difference in educational organization (1) when the criteria of decision-making in crucial areas of organization have been changed, and (2) when the bases of legitimacy for the organization have been shifted. Chapter iii presented some evidence on the first point, with program building by means of the sign-up list epitomizing the difference from regular school types. In this chapter, in a description of the relationship between the adult school and outside organizations, further evidence of this change will be presented. Then we shall take up the second point, the bases upon which this type of organization seeks acceptance and support.

COSPONSORING GROUPS

The special turn that service has taken in the last decade is service to particular groups and organizations. The adult program has increas-

[1] Los Angeles City School Districts, *Point of View*, no. 470, 1949.

ingly penetrated the organized group structure of the community—an adaptation that offers inexhaustible opportunities. Both private firms and public agencies need pre-job and on-the-job training of employees. Much of this vocational training may be brought under the adult education program, especially since the limits of school responsibility are blurred, and at the same time many firms are seeking school assistance. Voluntary associations such as service clubs and professional groups have membership activities or clientele services that can be feasibly organized in conjunction with the schools as adult classes.

Table 13 lists some of the many organizations cosponsoring classes with the Los Angeles adult schools early in 1953. This information came from mail questionnaire data; the sample included about one-sixth of the teachers in the adult education branch. With more than fifty cosponsored classes specified in the data, it may be inferred that at least three hundred were cosponsored in the period February–June, 1953. The actual total would be larger, since the questionnaire information is an underrepresentation.[2] Of the total number of classes reported on the questionnaire (318), fifty-eight, or 18.2 per cent, were listed as cosponsored. This figure approximates that found in a state-wide sample in 1948–49;[3] thus we may estimate that about one-fifth of the courses are connected with outside organizations. Appendix VIII shows a partial list of cosponsoring organizations that further displays the heterogeneity of such groups.

Cosponsored classes assume more importance than their numbers would indicate, since cosponsorship is useful to the adult school in a number of ways. To demonstrate what is involved in these ties to diverse organizations, we have broken down the cosponsorship pattern into several elements. The illustrative data came from interviews with five cosponsoring organizations.

ELEMENTS OF COSPONSORSHIP

ACCESS AND LEGITIMATION

When outside organizations support adult classes, the minimal elements

---

[2] Some cosponsorship would not be reported. Occasionally a respondent would not be sure whether an organizational tie was involved. More importantly, some respondents were risking trouble for themselves and their organization in answering the question. Cosponsorship was under scrutiny at the time in the investigation of the Senate Interim Committee on Adult Education and it may be expected that due caution was exercised by some respondents. For the committee's findings on cosponsorship, see their report (pp. 79–162).

[3] In the 1948–49 sample, 13 per cent of all classes were cosponsored, with 17 per cent cosponsored in large cities. Percentages computed from data in Philip M. Ferguson, "Practices in the Administration of Adult Education in the Public Schools of California," pp. 31, 71.

in the pattern of cosponsorship are access to clientele and some partial legitimation of courses. Nearly all the sponsoring agencies have their own channels of communication to internal membership or to their clientele. The organization may have a mailing list that would not be readily available to school personnel, such as sales executives, building

TABLE 13
COSPONSORING ORGANIZATIONS,
LOS ANGELES ADULT SCOOLS

Public Agencies
  California Department of Motor Vehicles
  County Government
  Los Angeles Civil Defense
  Los Angeles Public Housing Authority
  Olive View Sanitorium
  U. S. Immigration and Naturalization Service
  U. S. Navy
  U. S. Veterans Administration Hospital

Service Clubs and Associations
  Air Reserve
  Chambers of Commerce
  Contractors Association
  Jewish Women's Council
  Los Angeles and Glendale Lapidary Societies
  Officers' Wives and NCO Club, Fort MacArthur
  Parent-teacher associations
  Pasadena Hearing Society
  West Ebell Club

Business Concerns
  Lockheed Aircraft Corporation
  North American Aircraft Corporation

Labor Unions
  Die Sinkers Union
  Electricians Union
  Sheet Metal Union

Other
  Foundation for Exceptional Children
  Fund for Adult Education, Ford Foundation
  Salvation Army

SOURCE: Based on data from mail questionnaire. A partial list for February–June, 1953.

contractors, and retail business associations. The Medical Assistants' Association, for example, was able to make direct contacts with doctors' offices throughout Los Angeles by means of the records of the County Medical Association. (See Appendix IX for the form letter sent out by this group.) The Medical Assistants' Association also advertised its courses in medical publications. Parent-teacher associations have their own newspapers in which they advertise classes they are sponsoring, and they distribute mimeographed announcements at monthly meetings. Chambers of commerce issue pamphlets and place notices in newspapers. The cosponsoring groups make these contacts at their own expense.

An important factor is the time and energy that cosponsoring organizations put into the approach to clientele. The principal of a large adult school has many cosponsorships active at one time. Each of the outside cosponsors is carrying out some of the routine work entailed in reaching a specific public. An organization with an interest of its own in a course will take the "time to do the legwork and publicize the thing," as one respondent in a cosponsoring group put it, adding: "the principals could never publicize the way I can—and people receiving the mail think it is more basic if an organization in the field is sponsoring it." Assistance ranges from personal contacting to newspaper advertising. A chamber of commerce interviewee, when queried on the extent of his chamber's aid on a course, replied, "We just publicize it through our own media and the newspapers. Our whole responsibility was sponsoring it and advertising it."

A second minimal element is the lending of organizational prestige. Sometimes the name of the outside group appears on printed brochures and advertisements. The Department of Motor Vehicles formally sponsors driver education by lending its name in this manner. For potential students, such approval certifies a class and increases its drawing power. The chamber of commerce in effect places its stamp of approval on courses it is cosponsoring in investments or salesmanship. The prestige of the outside organization is reflected in small segments of the school program, with the possibility that this prestige may be generalized by the public to apply to the adult school as a whole, or at least to major parts of its operations.

PERSONNEL AND CONTENT

The second important aspect of cosponsorship centers in the securing of teachers and the determining of course content. The importance of the outside organization in these administrative domains tends to be proportional to the specialization of the subject matter. Where courses are highly specialized, the principals need to rely on expert judgment from outside groups. Several examples will illustrate the role of cosponsors in securing instructors and shaping content.

For the courses supported by the Medical Assistants' Association, the selection of teachers and the determination of content was principally in the hands of the association. From its inception this group had taken the training of medical assistants as one of its basic purposes. In 1952 the example of medical classes in another school system suggested the possibility of cosponsorship. The plan was approved, and the president of the association selected several instructors, who were allowed to determine course content and invite guest lecturers. The content was shaped also by audience suggestions in evaluation questionnaires at the end of the first course. The courses were very popular and spread to three adult schools. According to the association respondent, more than two hundred students turned out at the first session in 1952, and the following year applicants were turned away.

The cosponsoring of driver education classes by the Department of Motor Vehicles is a less sharply defined example. The department has chosen thus far to limit its formal participation in cosponsorship, but informally its members are very active. A majority of the driver education instructors in adult schools are from the department, and the original course outlines were developed by several department men operating informally as coördinators. From these outlines and through trial and error, a basic ten-night, three-hours-a-night course has evolved, on the revolving-membership pattern mentioned in chapter iii. Within this framework the instructors, as specialists in the Motor Vehicles Code and driver training, have considerable leeway in classroom technique and course organization. The principals do not interfere. The informal coördinators have been instrumental also in recruiting new men, since they know who is available within the department and reasonably competent.

RECRUITMENT AND ENROLLMENT

A third main aspect of cosponsorship is the direct recruitment of class members and the maintenance of class strength by the coöperating organization. This means going beyond access to clientele, the first element above, to direct involvement in class maintenance. Where the teacher comes from the cosponsoring group, he is typically most closely involved. Next to the teacher, the greatest interest in recruitment and enrollment is likely to be shown by officers of the outside association.

The prototype here is cosponsorship by parent-teacher associations and councils, the most active sponsors of adult classes. Parent education is an old, established function of the P.T.A., which holds its lower units responsible for activity in this field.[4] When an association holds classes or study groups on parent education, it receives credit from the higher council and district offices as part of an incentive system for leadership

---
[4] California Congress of Parents and Teachers, Inc., *Parent Education Manual, 1952–53*, pp. 5–8.

and effort at lower levels. When parent education classes are cosponsored with an adult school, a chairman is delegated to recruit students and attempt to maintain attendance. For example, four associations in a neighborhood may support one class. Each association provides a minimum of five in attendance in any one evening, assuring a class minimum of twenty. In order to meet the association's quota, the chairman contacts members. This includes direct appeals to individual members that the association "needs the credit" and that credit depends on attendance. When replacements are needed, the chairman tries to supply new recruits. In this way there is an amalgamation of interest between association officers and adult school administrators. The California Congress of Parents and Teachers defines compliance with board of education attendance requirements to be a "definite obligation" of sponsoring parent-teacher groups.[8]

Considering the dozens of classes supported during any one term in the Los Angeles system by the many parent-teacher associations, it is apparent that the school principals have a small army of association chairmen, publicity chairmen, and parent education chairmen acting as their administrative assistants. With enrollment reasonably guaranteed, the close tie with the P.T.A. is of major benefit. The day classes—parent education, homemaking, crafts—in particular tend to be supported by the P.T.A. The largest bloc of classes cosponsored by one organization is that of the P.T.A.; approximately 20 per cent of the cosponsored classes in the mail questionnaire data are P.T.A. classes.

Outside the P.T.A., cosponsorship usually does not include direct effort in maintaining enrollment. Occasional aid may be given by members of the outside group. Part of the relationship between the Motor Vehicles men and the driver education classes is that the instructors, through their regular daytime contacts with driver applicants, can refer students to each other's classes. And some organizations assist the schools by circulating sign-up lists and enrolling class members through their own offices.

EVALUATION

Cosponsors enter decisively into evaluation of class results, since it is crucial that they be satisfied. Officials may make their evaluation partly on the basis of word-of-mouth reports from class members and from their own observation. Or in vocational-business classes cosponsored by trade associations, the reaction of employers will be relayed to an association official and become a key element in evaluation. But there are no systematic, objective techniques available, and informal assessment must be backed by student enrollment. In the driver education

---

[8] *Ibid.*, p. 9.

classes, most students take a written test and proceed to the Department of Motor Vehicles for the driving test. But in other than the simplest type of class, evaluation of teacher, student, and course value is difficult and not systematically pursued.

These are aspects of the pattern of cosponsorship between adult schools and outside organizations: access to clientele, legitimation of courses, provision of teachers, determination of course content, maintenance of student enrollment, and evaluation of class results. Cosponsorship touches upon all the important aspects of course organization. In the extreme case of a job-training class given in an industrial plant or business office with an employee as instructor and other employees as students, class organization is very much in the hands of the cosponsoring agency. Usually, however, some effort devolves upon the school principal, and authority to continue or discontinue courses remains within the school. The cosponsorship pattern provides a diffusion of the work of program building from the principal's office out through the groups that are using the classes. The burdens of administration are shared with organized constituencies. This is a weak form of the process that has been labeled "formal coöptation"[9]—a process of absorbing outside groups into an organization in order to facilitate access to clientele and further the legitimation of an organization.

The coöptation pattern is weak in the adult school because of several factors. Most of the adult classes are a marginal activity of the cosponsoring associations, related to job training or an additional clientele service. The cosponsor can continue to operate quite well without the classes. Second, the job-training possibilities for a firm are soon exhausted. A cosponsor is often temporary, becoming used up after a specific service has been provided. The program is not pinned down by a long-term commitment to particular groups, with the important exception of the P.T.A.—and even here student clientele can be exhausted. Thus the cosponsorship pattern that links an adult school to organized groups in the community is somewhat unstable.

LONG-TERM ADVANTAGES OF COSPONSORSHIP

Adult administrators are aware of the potentialities in cosponsorship for gaining support in the community. The following quotation provides a good example of this awareness:

> The adult education program should recognize the needs and interests of groups which tend to give strength to the community. Leaders of industry, agriculture, commerce, labor, parent groups, service organizations, and other local agencies should be consulted for suggestions in formulating the program. As these leaders

---

[9] Philip Selznick, *TVA and the Grass Roots*, chap. vii.

understand that the adult education program will be formed or extended to meet the special needs and interests of their organization, they will coöperate in a manner that will greatly enrich the program. Courses sponsored and encouraged by community agencies are greatly benefited in terms of both attendance and opportunity to serve the public.[7]

The specific ways in which cosponsors aid the schools, other than in attendance, include operating as extensions of adult schools, which are able to reach a larger number of student groups through this radiating network. The mediating organizations actually differentiate the general adult population into blocs within which there is common interest, allowing the schools to adapt their fragmented programs to such groups. With the enormous complexity of interest found in the outside community, this adaptation can be highly developed. In-service training for specific firms has seemingly thus far permitted the greatest differentiation—as an extreme example, a class in gift-wrapping for the Christmas season employees of a department store. Thus, for the adult school, the organized group structure of the population is translatable as an organized clientele structure.

Besides linking adult schools to this clientele structure, cosponsorship gains support from centers of power in the city and state. Some of the groups served are loci of political power. Cosponsorship is public relations where it counts, functioning to neutralize hostile groups and to cement support for adult education. Adult-school administrators openly suggest that cosponsorship has been instrumental in turning opposition groups into supporters.[8] The chamber of commerce is an illuminating example. Local chambers of the state organization are autonomous, writing their own policy recommendations on civic and political issues. The cosponsoring of classes by local chambers tends to separate them from the attitude of their higher leadership on adult education: representatives of the chamber of commerce were, in 1952–53, at the state capitol supporting certain types of restriction on the program, but some chambers went on record as against these restrictions. The women's division of the Los Angeles Chamber of Commerce, together with the Los Angeles Stock Exchange, has cosponsored investment courses with the adult schools of Los Angeles. Some of these courses were held in movie theaters. At the same time, representatives of the Los Angeles Chamber of Commerce supported legislation at Sacramento that would bar classes not held on school property. Through

---

[7] State of California, Department of Education, *Bulletin*, 18, no. 4 (May, 1949), p. 16.

[8] "It is interesting to note that organizations which, not many years ago, were opposing the development of adult education in the state are now operating as cosponsors of classes." Ferguson, *op. cit.*, p. 70.

cosponsorship, local units thus become tied to the adult schools. When asked how cosponsored courses helped his organization, a chamber respondent replied, "Indirectly. It doesn't help us financially. But it is good public relations. The public realizes that we are trying to help them."

Over the long run, cosponsorship means that an adult school can establish a service relationship to most of the organized groups in its district. This is done directly through cosponsored classes. It is accomplished indirectly and symbolically by establishing the idea in the community that the adult program is a community program, potentially available for service to any organization.

THE NEED FOR LEGITIMACY

A review of administrative practice in the adult education branch suggests that the defining feature of the organization lies in its service to clientele. The program is other-directed rather than guided by a professional conception of what ought to be. Stimuli for program changes come from outside or from personnel who are aware of what would interest outside groups. The organization reacts rather than initiates.

Every organization strives to gain acceptance of its authority and activity, especially from groups significantly related to its welfare. With the service relationship now predominating, the adult school feels a particular need to legitimize its position.[*] For a marginal school program, acceptance is needed from various groups: other departments within the immediate school system, such state organizations as the California Teachers Association, the state legislature, and various segments of the general public.

On what basis does the organization seek legitimacy and with what consequences? Especially, when the pressure is on, as it was in the period 1951–1953 (see chap. v), how does the organization defend itself? In a context of concerted attack and vigorous defense, the practices of the schools have to be given a plausible rationale. Out of many statements made by adult administrators, it is possible to isolate three basic principles of legitimacy that have been widely used in attempting to gain acceptance for a service program.

1. *Adult education is a low-cost operation.* The seeds of this principle lie in the generous state support discussed in chapters i and ii. It is an argument used principally *within* school systems when the program

---

[*] Legitimacy is used throughout this analysis as a sociopsychological rather than a legal concept. It does not refer to the legality of organizational position and practice but to its acceptance by others. See Max Weber, *The Theory of Social and Economic Organization*, pp. 124–132; Herbert A. Simon, D. W. Smithburg, and V. A. Thompson, *Public Administration*, pp. 198–201.

must be defended before boards of education and other administrators. One point in the argument is that local districts do not have to spend much for the program, since it is covered in large part by state funds. A second point is that the program takes only 2 or 3 per cent of the school budget, and no substantial saving can be made by cutting into it. The greatest temptation to support the program in this way lies in districts where the program is most insecure and where, at the same time, it has more than paid for itself out of state funds. It is least used where the adult education men realize that acceptance on this basis is debilitating, for it perpetuates their marginality and undermines more ethical principles. State leaders have cautioned against this type of defense, urging that the program be defended on the ground of its intrinsic educational value.[10] In the Los Angeles system the principle is used infrequently and in a mild form. It is sometimes stressed that adult education is less expensive than the high school and junior college programs, with the implication that the program obtains greater returns per dollar of expense and is efficiently administered.[11] This argument has utility, especially when used in conjunction with the following two principles. But it is clear that this is a minimal-defense type of principle, tending to legitimize adult education at the margin.

2. *Adult education is a valuable public relations instrument for the entire school system.* This justification is of fundamental import, for it suggests that an adult school's service program gathers support from taxpayers and voters for the entire school system and not merely for itself. Used extensively by adult administrators in seeking support within school ranks, this is *the* core strategy whenever the administrators have to bargain with other levels for support. It is the cultivation of favorable public sentiment for the entire system through service to adult groups that the adult administrators present as a special contribution to the general welfare of the schools. The Bureau of Adult Education states the argument clearly:

Adults of the community who attend adult schools become friends of the entire school program....

Several times in recent years the adult citizens of California have been called upon to vote on measures which provide the legal bases for the financial support of public education in this State. These citizens have consistently supported constructive legislation by large popular majorities. It is impossible to measure the extent to which adult education contributed to this result, but it is known to have been

---

[10] Dr. George C. Mann, chief of the Bureau of Adult Education, has stressed this point in conferences and workshops of adult administrators.

[11] In Los Angeles in 1952–53, direct per capita costs were $365.44 for junior colleges, $349.82 for senior high schools, and $223.23 for adult schools. The adult administrators bring this comparison in expenses to the attention of the Board of Education.

substantial. *The best way to interest adults in the public school system is to make them a part of it.*[13] [Italics mine.]

The public relations value for the rest of the school system of service to organizations has been voiced also by a Los Angeles program coördinator:

> The Distributive Education classes offered to community organizations and business firms are, in many cases, the only tangible evidence that the businessman in the community has for the return of a part of his tax dollar. Here is concrete evidence in the form of service from the school itself.
>
> A part of the outstanding service that Distributive Education renders the Los Angeles Schools is in this very desirable form of public relations. During the course of a school year, school services are rendered to many community groups and business organizations from San Pedro to San Fernando, from large retail stores to groups of small businessmen.[13]

Such educational-defense organizations as the California Teachers Association realize that the adult-school program touches nearly a million adults a year in the state. The extent of actual support garnered for school systems is somewhat beside the point in analyzing the impact of the argument. The belief that the program operates in this manner is important in determining the way in which other educational groups and key state figures define the adult education situation.

The potentiality of the adult education program as a public relations tool is discussed in the literature of educational administration. A school administration text, for example, suggests seven instruments for public relations, only one of which is an operating school program—adult education.[14] For top administration, this instrumental use of the program can be a potent factor in winning acceptance for it. Public relations need to be kept in good repair, and when a school system is in a state of disequilibrium with the social forces around it, the restoration of balance becomes the basic concern of top administration. For a 2 per cent budget item, the service to the educational system of maintaining a workable equilibrium with the community is a realistic basis upon which to defend the adult-school program. The cost can be understood as a public relations expenditure.

3. That *adult education should be geared to public demand* is the most important of the legitimizing principles that has emerged in the development of the adult school. This philosophic doctrine has wide meaning

---

[12] *California Schools*, 22, no. 11 (November, 1951), pp. 402–403.
[13] William R. Hathaway, "Distributive Education—Economic Necessity," *Los Angeles School Journal*, 26, no. 5 (January 14, 1953), p. 14. "Distributive education" includes real estate selling, insurance selling, department store selling, wholesale selling, and general salesmanship.
[14] Jesse B. Sears, *Public School Administration*, p. 229.

and is used outside as well as within school ranks. The idea is frequently expressed that it is the public and not professional fiat that should decide program content. The concept of the adult school as a client-directed organization has been expressed by the former superintendent of the Los Angeles school system (Alexander J. Stoddard) in analogy with retail business: "These schools and classes are educational service stations for all the people." Statements of general purpose, as indicated in chapter ii, stress a curriculum based on the present needs and interests of the people. The principle is incorporated in so many public pronouncements of adult-school administrators that it may be said to represent the basic ground for gaining moral approval. It amounts to an interpretation by schoolmen of the role of adult education organizations in a democracy: the programs are tuned to public sentiment rather than imposed by professionals.

The service pattern is thus linked to the meaning of democracy, and a moral halo is given to program building by course popularity. With its democratic overtones, the doctrine of public demand has strength in a field where there is now much self-consciousness about democratic administration and community-school relations. Moreover, the principle is an important fighting tool, for it labels opponents of the service-type program as autocratic and arbitrary in their opposition to a people's program. In addition, it links directly to the interests of each student group. Each student bloc feels that its own interests are equal or superior to other interests as components of the program. The doctrine of public demand gives administrative sanction to the view that no courses have priority. All are equal, and their value is to be determined by strength of demand. In this way program administrators come to view their authority and practices as legitimized by public demand, defining this as appropriate for a democratic adult education program.

The justification of adult education as a low-cost operation has a utility that varies through time and from one area to another. It depends upon the method of state support. The second and third principles, however, seem endemic in service-type adult education. Together they define an ideology of service. The public-relations justification stresses the instrumental role of adult education for the rest of the school system; the public-demand principle, its service to the people. While the emphasis upon the three principles shifts with their tactical use in different situations, the ideology of service constitutes a permanent administrative doctrine for schools exhibiting the service pattern of organization-clientele relationship. Legitimacy, in the eyes of adult administrators and teachers and in the view of others convinced by these rationales, becomes based on the public-demand principle more than on any other single premise. The emergent service ideology *sanctions* the emergence of an amorphous "cafeteria" program.

Earlier it was suggested that the grounds upon which an organization defends its position and practices are indicative of its basic orientation. The foregoing principles shift the question of legitimate program building away from professional assessment of educational import. The idea that acceptance ought to be granted on the basis of internal evaluation may be construed as the traditional principle of legitimacy for school programs. The elementary and high school levels have been able to claim, in effect, that they are important and proper activities of the schools because of their intrinsic educational worth in the rearing of the young. Their programs are considered to be professionally set, and changes are defended as stemming from professional research and experimentation. The evolution of curriculum and teaching practices is considered a matter for the judgment of experts. There is much concern with defending the principle of professional control against lay intervention.

In contrast, the use of these three principles in adult education shifts acceptability away from the traditionalist premise. Intrinsic educational value has sometimes been attributed to adult education, but rather apologetically. Since the adult administrators are responsible for what the adult schools do, they feel compelled to defend the educational value of *all* their courses and practices. This breaks the traditional ethic down into a relativistic one, that every course has value for some group of adults. This position then becomes subsumed under the doctrine of giving the people what they want.

The organizational meaning of the principles of legitimacy is clear. The adult education units do not define themselves as schools wherein educators determine standards and critically differentiate between competing subject matters. Acceptance for a different type of school is sought on service premises. That this be so, in our interpretation, is determined in large part by the organizational pressures generated by the conditions of existence.

Chapter V

CONTINUING INSECURITIES

Efforts to reduce the vulnerability of the adult school have taken the form of attempting to end its marginal status. Hence the great concern of administrators with gaining acceptance, and the time and energy put into selling the program. If the adult schools were private ventures, they would be relatively free to make their own rules of conduct. At least they would have no need to cast themselves in a public school mold, and would probably be less hampered by the judgments of professional educators. But this is mere conjecture. The adult schools are part of the public school system and must stand judgment by educators and the public on this basis.

The adult program is expected to be "educational" and worthy of public funds. And what is educational and valuable is defined by historically derived norms and values. The behavior of teachers and administrators at other school levels is governed by relatively stable expectations in the school and in the community. Although these norms arose from and are centered around the education of the young, they are generally transferred to the adult school. A course is expected to have an educational rationale; teachers should transmit knowledge and skill to students at a high rate of return on the school dollar; teachers should not be too adaptive to student demands; history and mathematics are more legitimate than hobbies as subject matter; administrators are to be professional program builders, articulating and integrating courses into meaningful curricular patterns.

The adult-school administrators cannot ignore these traditional norms, no matter how much they may feel their work misunderstood. Since it is so important to them that marginality be reduced, the judgment of established groups on proper behavior becomes a crucial matter. It is not surprising, therefore, that the work of the adult administrators must be aligned with a *logic of respectability*, as defined by existing norms of proper educational practice. To put it bluntly, the service program must face up to the school context. Hence the dilemma of the adult school: Are the administrators to follow the logic of an out-and-out service program, as it is propelled by the demands of the enrollment economy, or should they allow themselves to be guided by general school norms, gaining acceptance by doing the traditionally proper thing? This dilemma is no trivial matter, since it is formed by conflicting organizational needs. In general, *the short-run needs of the enrollment economy are incompatible with the long-run need of obtaining educational respectability.* Survival and security in the short run depend upon budget and clientele; but over the long run these basic needs can be effectively met only by assuming an accepted, morally legitimate school role. The latter type of organizational need can no more be ignored than can the immediate needs. When it is ignored, the price is continuing insecurity.

The importance of legitimacy, always latent in the thinking of the adult administrators, is brought home sharply when the program is under concerted attack. Then the need for educational respectability becomes pressing and the dilemma is intensified. Operating pressures, reënforced by the emergent service ideology, continually bring into the program the very practices most difficult to defend as possessing educational value. Where open-ended purpose provides no anchoring point, the program drift becomes a source of administrative embarrassment. Adult administrators are held accountable, as a group, for practices that even within the ranks are considered undesirable. They well know that such classes as those in yacht-repairing or dog-training are troublemakers. But these experiments are difficult to prevent; authority is decentralized, and control standards are weakly established. Thus there is some resistance from within adult education to unwanted programs, but it is rarely implemented.

There is also some resistance from other school levels to the service program, a resistance, however, that does not usually come to public view. Educators are reluctant to speak out against any one of the school programs. The schools have enough trouble without their own personnel providing ammunition for outside critics, and a premium is placed upon organizational loyalty. But from members of the State Board of Education down to teachers there is deep concern over the tendency of the adult school to adopt an extreme service position. Informal interviewing of school personnel in the state structure[1] indicates that sizable portions of the program are considered inappropriate for the public school. Arts and crafts, some homemaking courses, dancing, and sports ranked low; unacceptable also were lecture series of large enrollment, movies, and highly specialized classes for specific firms and service clubs—in general, the recreational type of program, and classes related to private clienteles.

In the light of such subjects and practices, known to school personnel, the service ideology does not fully serve as a program rationale.

---

[1] State Board of Education, State Department of Education, high school and junior college administrators (in and about Los Angeles), high school and junior college teachers (Los Angeles), adult education personnel (in and about Los Angeles), headquarters administrators and board of education members of the Los Angeles school system.

The low-ranking components cause a disproportionate amount of trouble, rendering it difficult to get service rules of conduct firmly established and morally sanctioned. Others persist in pinpointing these elements as lacking in educational value. The practices of low repute tend to discount or corrupt the service model, since they are viewed as improper and indicative of administrative expediency. Such critical judgments by other schoolmen reënforce the still existent tendency within adult education to question the educational value of its program. Many adult teachers express strong disapproval of square-dancing, or of the instructor who fills class hours with movies, or of classes provided for a specific firm. From many quarters the traditional ethics of education seriously hamper the establishing of an uninhibited service facility.

Resistance to the service mode of conduct not only takes the form of occasional ridicule from other schoolmen and passive refusal to accept it, but at times breaks into an open counterattack—an effort to fence in the program drift. Such offensives are usually initiated outside the school system by conservative interest groups and the state legislature. Then covert assistance from within the educational hierarchy may be perceived. An examination of the controversy over adult education in the state during the period 1951-1953 will help us gauge the effect of traditional resistance upon the adult school. This conflict may be assessed in terms of program legitimacy and organizational insecurity.

ATTACK FROM THE LEGISLATURE

A Senate interim committee on adult education played a key part in a recent offensive against the program. The committee was established in June, 1951, to study adult education "conducted under the average daily attendance (A.D.A.) program of the State."[2] It took as its purpose "a review of the current program and the State's ability to finance adult education at present along with the other responsibilities of State government."[3] The committee studied state apportionments, surveyed one hundred thirty-four local programs, and conducted interviews and hearings throughout the state. From the start it was clear that the committee disapproved of many adult-school practices. The senators were interested in economy and an explicit platform of standards for whatever adult education was to be charged to state funds. The committee challenged the program as one having too many "frills," with

---

[2] State of California, *Partial Report of the Senate Interim Committee on Adult Education*, 1953, p. 7.
[3] *Ibid.*

some 55 per cent of adult enrollment in the state falling into this category.[4] Attracting considerable public attention, the investigation was conducted from the first in the atmosphere of an exposé. The committee, with its sharply critical approach, became a powerful organized center through which opposition to the program could be funneled. Because of its investigatory power, the committee was in a position to deal out punishment. For one thing, the hearings in all parts of the state gave the committee a "watchdog" character. The adult administrators of the state, even before the committee went into action, foresaw that it would recommend legislation outlawing certain practices and precipitating retrenchment. From its inception in the spring of 1951 the committee exerted a strong counterpressure against the adult program.

The adult-school administrators were challenged to decide on the tactics of their common defense. One response was the instituting of program policing in an effort to get rid of the least defensible practices and thus "pull the teeth" of the inquiry. The administrators proceeded to review their own programs and to discontinue suspect classes. It was understood that the administrators were to be on their best behavior. The program changes might have come about naturally at some later time, but it is clear that they were precipitated in the last half of 1951 by the threat of the investigation. When heavy pressure is on, program reform is a common means of organizational protection.

To accomplish the formal changes, the state administrative regulations were virtually rewritten in July and November, 1951. The sections of the California *Administrative Code* that pertained to adult education were modified and new sections added.[5] Greater formal authority for control over local programs was given to the State Department's Bureau of Adult Education. New standards were instituted on crafts (limiting the number of hours that students could stay in one

---

[4] "Classes in this group were art classes with the exception of certain commercial and advertising art, china painting, textile painting and crafts; interior decorating, sculpturing, ceramics; sewing and allied crafts such as draperies, bed spreads, slipcovers, knitting, crocheting, all of which appeared more avocational than vocational; flower arrangement; jewelry, leathercrafts and hobbycrafts; photography, upholstery, weaving, rug making, woodwork and miscellaneous crafts such as cake decorating and Christmas gift wrapping; little theater and assorted drama classes; forums and discussion groups, lecture; cooking and home economics classes of the avocational type; courses for persons in the military reserve pertaining to military procedures; all music; all physical education, including folk dancing and other dancing; certain psychology classes devoted to personal development; psychology of personal grooming, etc.; first aid and civil defense courses; and certain miscellaneous classes such as dog obedience training and fish and game reserve wardens." *Ibid.*, pp. 171–172.

[5] State of California, *Administrative Code*, 1951, Title 5, secs. 118–129.1. Every section of Article 14, "Evening Schools and Classes for Adults," became an amendment or a new section, dated July 21, 1951, and November 1, 1951.

course), on classes for organizations ("Classes for adults shall not be held as part of meetings of clubs or organizations"), on classes held at military bases (classes limited to nonmilitary courses), on the use of films, and on prohibition of classes for purely recreational purposes. Actually, the increase in effective control over local schools was relatively small, for compliance remained a matter of voluntary submission to the spirit of the state regulations. The Bureau of Adult Education is undermanned, it does not have a corps of field inspectors, and the State Department of Education is not oriented toward strong state control. The doctrine of local autonomy is ideologically viable in California, and is sustained by the power alignment: a weak state department, with power in the hands of local systems and associations manned by local administrators and teachers. The stiffening of rules "on the books," however, was a step toward establishing statewide control over program practices.

Thus the immediate effect of the committee was to increase counterpressures so much in the form of public exposé and threatened legislation that strong incentives were provided for changes made from within. To ward off intervention of the state legislature and further damage to reputation, the program had to give a little to the pressures exerted against it.

The second type of defense by adult-school administrators was a vigorous public stand, defending the program as legitimate. Closing ranks tightly, the administrators refused to criticize one another's work in committee testimony, and defended virtually all classes as educational and (or) in accordance with public demand. In this defense, the service ideology was intertwined with traditional premises of educational worth. The administrators had no choice here: either they must defend courses as having educational value or else admit that other criteria were sometimes used in decision-making. Legitimacy had to be based on educational worth. The belief that schools ought to "educate" is a community expectation that evidently cannot be ignored.

With this strong verbal defense against the committee's probing, however, went a vigorous effort to rally supporters, both for favorable testimony at committee hearings and for political support at the 1953 session of the state legislature. The first type of defense, the slight internal program policing, did not basically alter the adult school's relationship to its clientele. The service orientation is a defining characteristic of the schools and hence is not readily changed. It is not surprising that the second type of effort become the major tactic—a firm doctrinal defense of service programs and the mobilizing of supporters for a political contest on this basis.

In the struggle that followed, during the 1953 session of the state legislature, adult education was at times only a football in a contest between the California Senate and the California Teachers Association. The senators voted overwhelmingly for a heavily restrictive bill; the crucial battle was fought in the Assembly, where the C.T.A. has strong influence. But even in what seem pure power struggles, the pros and cons of the issues are never completely lost. And it was here that the report of the Senate committee constituted documentation of waste[6] in the program, considerably heightening the pressure upon educational groups to agree to major changes in state regulations. In the context of the committee's report and the severe committee-sponsored bill, the state educational forces submitted compromise legislation, and then had to battle in the Assembly to prevent the passage of the most restrictive measures. Top school administrators made no attempt to bargain for maximum protection of the present program, but started off by incorporating many of the Senate's recommendations into their own school-sponsored Assembly bills. This was both the better part of political valor, in the context of the Senate report, and an expression of the belief within top school ranks that the program needed some restricting. In this way a number of program restrictions were passed. Standards for approval of courses by the State Department of Education were more closely specified, adult attendance was taken out of the computing of equalization funds, in-service training for specific firms was circumscribed, and an attempt was made to rule out recreation.[7]

Underlying the entire controversy was the issue of what constitutes an acceptable program for support by state funds. The committee's attitude epitomized the strict traditionalist view that the program should be limited to specifiable categories under close professional control. From this point of view the open-ended type of program appeared to be governed by nothing more than rank expediency. Moderate forms of this stand were held within educational ranks. But some of the adult administrators went to the opposite extreme: "tiddlywinks" should be allowed in the program if people want it.

What the 1951–1953 investigation did, in this context, was not so

---

[6] The term "waste" was used by the California Teachers Association in describing its attitude toward the proposed restrictive legislation. *CTA Journal*, 49 (April, 1953), p. 13.

[7] These restrictions became expressed in changes in the *Education Code* (effective September 9, 1953), secs. 7097–7098, 9700.1–9708, 9751–9755; and in the *Administrative Code*, Title 5, secs. 118–129.8.

much to convert those believing in a service program as to force changes by intensifying the need for educational respectability. This need varies according to the intensity of criticism. When an aroused lay opposition publicly denounced practices that the administrators themselves found indefensible, some measure of program control was inevitable. The expansion generated by service tendencies was boxed in, at least temporarily, and the program had to be reduced in size and scope. Top schoolmen, locally and at the state level, were constrained to discontinue courses that were both embarrassing and strongly opposed. In the context of open-ended purpose and weak program norms, the fastest and most effective way of discrediting school practice is to show that it has lost relevance to "education."

Since control by internal standards has been weak, the challenge from lay quarters has proved the main source of program control. Moreover, the lack of internal control invites such intervention from the outside. Lay groups may manipulate the incentives for changes within the professional hierarchy, but this external source of control is spasmodic in its efforts and effects. The state legislature has attempted to build control into the adult program, but, in the face of the pressures of the enrollment economy and the sentiments of the present administrative corps, such regulation has been largely ineffectual. Effective control must be sustained from *within* the school system; but in the decentralized and complicated state system the attempt has become worth while only when outside groups force the issue.

The 1951–1953 investigation of the adult education program in California highlights the difficulty the adult school has had in attaining a reputable status under its triple handicap of marginality, open-ended purpose, and severe enrollment economy pressures. The rules of administrative conduct that have emerged within the service organizations are not compatible with gaining acceptance on traditional grounds. The administrators have tried to justify their practices by means of the ideology of service, but they must contend with the traditional principle that each course should be judged on its relative educational merits. The latter means program building on the basis of professional discrimination among endless subject-matter alternatives.

The adult school has ridden out sustained attacks before, and seemingly has gradually strengthened its popular support and political power within the educational hierarchy. Its own principles of legitimacy have some acceptance, and external lay authority can only partially hem it in. But unless the opposition groups can rewrite the financial laws that provide internal incentives for a service facility, the basic character of the adult school remains unaffected. The state legislature may threaten the adult school's legitimacy and perpetuate its marginal status, but it cannot directly supervise the program nor divert it from a service orientation. The adult school survives such pressures; but its position is not strengthened thereby.

A more fundamental threat to the adult school now comes from an internal source rather than from such external ones. This is the expansion of the junior college into adult education. If we wish to understand the basic sources of continuing insecurity for the adult school, we must briefly discuss the California junior college. For it is in defending the adult school enterprise against the junior college expansion that the perpetuation of marginality becomes most injurious. Where attacks from the legislature, interest groups, and some educators reverse the process of legitimation, the adult school is more vulnerable to competition from other school departments. The likelihood is enhanced that other educational levels will become the chosen instruments of public-school adult education, with school funds and popular support going to them. Clientele groups do not seem intensely loyal to particular adult schools, but rather are attached to the notion of having interesting classes provided at convenient locations. The junior college now claims it can provide such a service better than can the adult school.

COMPETITION FROM COMMUNITY COLLEGES

In Los Angeles the adult education program has traditionally belonged to the adult school. Only one junior college existed prior to 1945. But since World War II and especially since 1948, an expanding junior college system has made deep penetrations into this province. This move parallels what has been happening elsewhere in the junior college. Increasingly, adult education has been defined as a proper extension of the several major junior college programs. Junior college functions have traditionally been a two-year university-parallel program for students transferring to four-year colleges and universities, and a program of two years of vocational training for students, terminating with an Associate of Arts degree. The terminal program for young people of eighteen to twenty-one is generally considered the unique purpose of the junior college, particularly in California.[9] Students attend a college for various lengths of time, frequently dropping out upon obtaining employment. Some appear for only a few courses,

---

[9] See the 1948 Strayer Report, *A Report of a Survey of the Needs of California in Higher Education*, pp. 6–7.

especially those already employed and taking night courses as preparation for better positions. In the vocational programs, many students have part-time and highly transitory ties to the colleges. Although the colleges were originally defined as secondary schools for youth who had completed high school, there have been no age restrictions. Under these conditions it was a natural evolution that, in broadening the scope of their activities, the junior colleges should develop specialized courses available to an all-age adult clientele. Today it is not uncommon for the student population of a junior college to be mainly over twenty-one, and for the college to be committed to a host of short-term courses similar to the adult school pattern.

Partly as cause and partly as effect of program extensions, a movement has developed within junior college circles for the broadening of the colleges into community colleges.⁹ The core idea in this conception is that program services should be greatly expanded in order to provide many classes needed by the community. A community college spokesman explains:

> What, then, is a community college and what did the President's Commission on Higher Education have in mind when the term was used? The first qualification is *service* primarily to the people of the community. The community institution goes to the people who live and work where it is located, makes a careful study of the needs of these people for education not being offered by any other institution of learning, analyzes these needs, and builds its educational program in response to the analyses.[10]

The junior college no longer need define itself as a two-year school or feel restricted by traditional self-definitions. It is to be a new type of educational enterprise, related to adults and filling many educational gaps. The pronouncements on purpose stress that the community college will be a service organization in much the same sense that the adult school has become a service agency. While the foregoing quotation seems to indicate a desire for professional assessment and planning, advocacy typically moves toward a service position. The community college leader quoted above has indicated: "It is not for the colleges and other schools to attempt to give the people what the colleges think they ought to have; it is for the people to decide for themselves what they want."[11] At the extreme this means in practice that "we will teach anyone, anywhere, anything, at any time whenever there are enough people interested in the program to justify its offering."[12]

---

⁹ For the history and advocacy of the community college movement see Jesse P. Bogue, *The Community College, passim.*
[10] *Ibid.*, p. 21.
[11] *Ibid.*, p. 225.
[12] *Ibid.*, p. 215.

The move toward a redefinition of the junior college has behind it not only this doctrine promulgated by adherents, but very real operating pressures as well. The development of adult constituencies represents, among other things, a means of filling enrollment gaps when such emergencies as military drafts threaten the very existence of a college, a means of building community support, and a basic means of organizational expansion. In a prolonged manpower draft such as that of World War II, a substitute student body must be found if a college is to continue to operate and to hold together a teaching staff.[13] During the draft of young men in 1950 and 1951, many junior colleges were confronted with this problem.

Of no less importance as a practical pressure for community college development is the public support to be gained by broadening the activities of the college. The junior college literature is replete with the suggestion that service begets support. The following statement by the executive secretary of the American Association of Junior Colleges puts it clearly:

> Even if the college is thinking only in terms of enlightened self-interest, its services to adults can be, as they have proved to be in many communities, one of the surest and soundest ways to build strong and favorable public relations. Many of the problems now facing public-school systems owing to the indifference of taxpayers could be resolved by services to the adults of the community.[14]

The operating pressures conducive to absorbing adult education into the junior college are often especially severe when a junior college system is new and is attempting a rapid expansion. New physical plants must begin to pay their way in student attendance, regardless of outside changes in employment levels and military drafts. And unless expansion is very carefully planned and timed, some of the facilities are initially premature; the expected student body does not materialize and administrators have to find additional clientele sources. Such pressures have been operative in the rapid expansion of the junior college system in Los Angeles since 1945 and especially since 1948.

Until 1945, there was one junior college, the Los Angeles City College; in 1945 a second was established, the East Los Angeles Junior College; in 1947 a third, the Pierce School of Agriculture; in 1949 a fourth and fifth, Valley Junior College and Harbor Junior College; and in 1949 and 1950 the main trade and business schools of the school

---

[13] Bogue has indicated that the category of "special and adult students" has had the greatest expansion in junior colleges throughout the country since 1938, with California setting the pace. This category reached its peak during World War II, amounting to 60 per cent of total enrollment in 1944. *Ibid.*, p. 35.

[14] *Ibid.*, p. 229.

system were moved into the junior college district (the Trade-Technical Junior College and Metropolitan Junior College). In 1952-53 the junior college system was composed of these seven colleges, six having been founded within the last ten years. Of these, Trade-Technical and Metropolitan have retained the trade and business-school character that

TABLE 14

STUDENT ENROLLMENT, DAY AND EVENING DIVISIONS, LOS ANGELES JUNIOR COLLEGES, SEPTEMBER, 1951

College	Day		Evening		Total	
	Number	Per cent	Number	Per cent	Number	Per cent
Los Angeles City College.............	5,550	39.9	8,373	60.1	13,923	100.0
East Los Angeles Junior College.............	2,135	50.2	2,116	49.8	4,251	100.0
Harbor Junior College...	1,332	65.9	690	34.1	2,022	100.0
Valley Junior College...	910	51.6	853	48.4	1,763	100.0
Metropolitan Junior College............:	804	19.1	3,401	80.9	4,205	100.0
Trade-Technical Junior College.............	1,924	35.8	3,450	64.2	5,374	100.0
Pierce School of Agriculture..........	420	24.1	1,321	75.9	1,741	100.0
Total.............	13,075	39.3	20,204	60.7	33,279	100.0

SOURCE: Los Angeles City School Districts, Division of Extension and Higher Education, *Junior Colleges*, January 7, 1952.

they possessed when they were part of the high school structure. They do not offer university-parallel work, but give an Associate of Arts degree in their terminal vocational programs. Their large evening divisions have tended to retain an adult-education definition of their activity. The Pierce School has a somewhat similar character, combining terminal agricultural training for relatively few full-time students with a large adult education evening division. The relative size of the enrollments in the day and evening sections of these colleges may be seen in table 14. A comparison of full-time and part-time student enrollments is shown in table 15.

The other four colleges give university-parallel courses as well as terminal vocational curricula and general adult education classes. Of these, the East Los Angeles Junior College has most sharply defined itself as a community college. This self-definition has meant an attempt to service directly a wide range of occupational groups and organizations with classes for their employees and members. E.L.A.J.C. has branch locations at the city hall, on the property of public utilities, at the county hospital, and in several high schools where there are adult schools. An excerpt from the E.L.A.J.C. general catalogue presented in Appendix X suggests the aims and tendencies of such a college.

The seven junior colleges became formally organized as a wing of the Division of Extension and Higher Education in 1950. A head-

TABLE 15
FULL AND PART-TIME STUDENT ENROLLMENT, LOS ANGELES JUNIOR COLLEGES, FALL, 1953

College	Full-time		Part-time		Total	
	Number	Per cent	Number	Per cent	Number	Per cent
Los Angeles City College..............	4,938	29.8	11,635	70.2	16,573	100.0
East Los Angeles Junior College.......	1,796	30.9	4,009	69.1	5,805	100.0
Harbor Junior College .	674	26.4	1,883	73.6	2,557	100.0
Valley Junior College ..	1,495	47.8	1,635	52.2	3,130	100.0
Metropolitan Junior College..............	460	9.9	4,203	90.1	4,663	100.0
Trade-Technical Junior College..............	2,337	32.9	4,777	67.1	7,114	100.0
Pierce School of Agriculture..........	356	14.3	2,136	85.7	2,492	100.0
Total..............	12,056	28.5	30,278	71.5	42,334	100.0

SOURCE: Computed from data contained in U. S. Department of Health, Education, and Welfare, Office of Education, *Resident, Extension and Adult Education Enrollment in Institutions of Higher Education, November, 1953* (Washington, D.C., 1954), pp. 7-8.

quarters junior college office was set up as a coördinating unit for the expanding system. Thus there has grown up alongside the adult education branch, within the same operating division, a second administrative structure which may be termed the junior college organization. In a very real sense this is a competitive organization for jurisdiction over adult education, and the adult administrators define the situation in this way. Like the adult schools, most of the new junior colleges relate themselves to widespread consumer interests and the needs of specific groups.[16] Like the adult schools, they tend to define their relationship

[16] There is considerable variation among the junior colleges of Los Angeles and the state in self-definition of purpose and proper activity. In Los Angeles, Valley Junior College has not been as strongly oriented toward community service courses

to the general population in terms of service. Crucial for our analysis is the fact that with the spread of their community service courses, junior colleges absorb adult education. This includes *abolishing the adult education label.* Junior college men in the state make it clear that they see no reason to earmark portions of their expanding programs as adult education.[15] Adult education becomes absorbed into the community college structure as junior college classes for part-time students. Where junior colleges and adult schools exist together within one school system or are in geographical proximity, these definitions clearly confront the adult schools and their own definitions of purpose and clientele.

In the competitive situation that has emerged in Los Angeles since 1948, the junior colleges have had some definite advantages. For one, Superintendent Alexander J. Stoddard, who assumed his position that year, was interested in the community college movement. Several informants reported that Dr. Stoddard construed one of his basic missions in the Los Angeles system, if not *the* mission, to be the building of a large system of community colleges, including four-year ones if possible. Such an interest would naturally include preferential treatment for the colleges. Also, the high school district within which adult schools were financed reached a tax-rate limit about this time, while the financial structure of the junior college district provided room for expansion. This played a part in the decision to transfer the trade and business schools into the junior college system in 1949 and 1950. With this move, the junior college organization moved well past the adult schools in the size, power, and importance of total activity. The overall growth of the Los Angeles junior college system since 1935–36 may be seen in table 16. The size of junior college average daily attendance in 1952–53 compared to that of adult schools was 20,277 to 11,176. The direct expense of operations was $7,000,000 compared to $2,500,000.[17]

As the junior college expansion continued, with a tendency toward junior college classes for part-time students, adult-school principals sought a clarification of administrative jurisdictions. Conflicts were

---

as East Los Angeles Junior College. Valley, seemingly, has attempted to work within preconceived patterns which set program limits. On the whole, however, the providing of service courses in response to unrelated consumer interests has been on the increase.

[16] Testimony of junior college administrators: "We try not to make any differentiation between our regular junior college classes and our adult program"; "I have only to add that our emphasis in the future is to do away with the term 'adult' as much as we possibly can"; "We want it clear we do not operate adult education as an adult program—we offer junior college classes for part-time students." *Partial Report of the Senate Interim Committee on Adult Education,* 1953, pp. 157, 311–312.

[17] Board of Education of the City of Los Angeles, *Controller's Annual Financial Report for the Fiscal Year Ending June 30, 1953.*

developing between adult schools and the colleges in regard to overlapping subject-matter areas and clientele. Junior college evening classes began to appear in high schools where adult schools normally had had control of classroom space. As the established party, the adult schools defined the colleges as raiders. The adult administrators, therefore, pressed for a top policy decision that would separate jurisdictions and protect the adult school province. But no such policy was forthcoming. And in the context of old adult schools and new junior colleges, the fact that top administration took no definite stand amounts

TABLE 16

GROWTH OF LOS ANGELES JUNIOR COLLEGE DISTRICT, AS
MEASURED BY UNITS OF AVERAGE DAILY ATTENDANCE

School year	A.D.A.	School year	A.D.A.
1935–36	4,544	1945–46	3,920
1936–37	4,421	1946–47	10,457
1937–38	4,321	1947–48	12,397
1938–39	5,281	1948–49	13,149
1939–40	5,702	1949–50	19,457
1940–41	4,873	1950–51	20,311
1941–42	4,118	1951–52	21,026
1942–43	3,143	1952–53	20,277
1943–44	2,648		
1944–45	2,414		

SOURCE: Los Angeles School System, Budget Division, *Financial Data* (annual reports).

to an informally set policy favoring the newer group. The school superintendent and the associate superintendent in charge of the Division of Extension and Higher Education have left the situation wide open, that is, with no definition of separate provinces for the two types of school. This is expressed as an administrative attitude of headquarters: the developing situation is experimental, and therefore headquarters should not attempt to establish a pattern upon it; the field chiefs should be "given their heads." The consequence is that the adult schools cannot protect their programs and constituencies against penetration by the colleges. Adult-school administrators feel that not only is their own province being invaded, but also they are being held back from fair combat by budget limitations.

Vocational education, a large and legitimate component of the adult program over a long period of time, is particularly susceptible to absorption into the expanding junior college framework. Harbor Junior College, established in 1949 in the southwestern section of Los Angeles, was equipped with machine shops that brought it into direct competition with several adult schools in that sector similarly equipped. Both full-time and part-time students were attracted to the college's facilities. But since a large full-time student body did not materialize, Harbor was under pressure to orient itself toward a part-time adult clientele. Several other junior colleges have had similar expansion problems, particularly the Pierce School of Agriculture. Vocational training for part-time students is a natural subject-matter area for the extended-day divisions of all the colleges. As blocs of trade and business courses stabilize, they are likely to be absorbed as junior college classes. Student groups like the status and credit possibilities of college courses, and the cosponsoring vocational groups find prestige value in the "higher education" label. But vocational courses are not the only ones subject to competing jurisdictions. The evening divisions of the colleges provide a wide range of service courses, many of which are similar to adult classes (e.g., sewing, photography, gardening).

The community college development thus directly affects the welfare of the adult school, which fears that its program may be cut out from under it by the rival administrative structure. This internal threat to security is even more basic than the threat of legislative curtailment. The junior college has a powerful base of operations, with permanent day programs connecting it to the high school and the university. It is an important part of the educational sequence, for a "wave of the future" is moving up in the form of large numbers of students now passing through the lower grades. For the colleges, adult education represents a program extension; the organizational hard core centers on programs that involve full-time students and full-time teachers. But the broadening of the colleges into community colleges means for the adult-school administrators the possible loss of most if not all of their domain. Without clear-cut directives to separate jurisdictions, the school system has two adult education vehicles which are increasingly competitive.

Such a dual structure usually generates an interest on the part of some in top positions to effect a consolidation for reasons of economy and effective administration. Several members of the Los Angeles Board of Education in 1952–53 considered the possibility of abolishing the adult education branch and transferring major responsibility for adult education to the junior colleges, with a few segments of the program reverting to high school administration. It is a top-level problem to decide whether to disband the adult schools, to pull adult education out of the junior colleges, to draw jurisdictional lines, or to permit a natural evolution to decide the situation.

Here the service character of the adult school has unanticipated consequences for its ability to defend and maintain itself. Its open-ended purpose provides little protection against penetration by other schools. Open-endedness means that the province of the adult school is not clearly defined; hence it is difficult to maintain the separateness of its business from that of bordering units. This point is particularly applicable to large school systems which include a number of junior colleges and adult schools. Therefore, while a broad conception of adult education has many functional consequences for the adult school (e.g., enlarging the scope of administrative discretion, broadening the sources of clientele, allowing rapid adaptation to environmental changes), a major dysfunction[18] is a reduced immunity to invasion by competing organizations. There is no clearly delineated content or clientele to which the adult school can claim exclusive rights. Without an established tradition of its province, there is no moral defense against the interest of the junior college in adult education. The lack of sanctioned program boundaries makes the adult school, the weaker party of the two, especially vulnerable. In situations similar to the one in Los Angeles, the adult school bids fair to become an organization without an activity or to be subsumed under junior college administration, unless it receives strong support from top local and state administration.

The issues may be reformulated as a problem of "specialization among organization units."[19] Adult-school principals want a division of work that will place all adult education in one unit, separate from other school activities. To achieve this end, they have come to emphasize specialization by clientele within the school system: "The human clientele to be served is what makes the difference in setting up various kinds of schools and segments and adults deserve schools and segments of their own."[20] Specialization on this basis would protect the adult school from the competition of the junior college. In fact, the above-quoted statement was an answer to "the idea so frequently put forth by some junior college spokesmen that adult education should not be

---

[18] *"Functions* are those observed consequences which make for the adaptation or adjustment of a given system; and *dysfunctions,* those observed consequences which lessen the adaptation or adjustment of the system." Robert K. Merton, *Social Theory and Social Structure,* p. 50.

[19] Cf. Herbert A. Simon, D. W. Smithburg, and V. A. Thompson, *Public Administration,* chap. vii.

[20] Bureau of Adult Education, *Report and Proceedings of the Montecito Workshop in Adult Education,* 1952, pp. 81-82.

recognized as such, but merely be blanketed in with education for lower-division college or older secondary students. . . ."[21] This program emphasis would enhance the stability of the adult schools because all adults would come to them. The community college movement, however, breaks down this specialization by clientele, and incorporates adults within the college province. The emphasis is upon specialization by educational levels (junior college education for part-time students), with the junior college free to tap adults as well as high school graduates.[22] Hence the tendency within the colleges is not to give adult education a separate identity. The junior colleges now offer school systems the possibility not only of transferring adult education into the junior college system, but of doing away with it entirely as a separate category.

The rise of a competitive structure presents an alternative for top administrators who take a skeptical view of the value of the adult-school program and dislike the orientation of the present administrative corps. A minority of them feel that perhaps the junior college can do better; that is, it may establish a pattern on the adult education program and control its development. Where the adult school develops classes and practices of low acceptance, it becomes vulnerable to such a major change. In this way it may lose more of its province to the junior college because of a lack of legitimacy. This seems most likely to come about as a slow erosion. Where the transfer becomes sufficiently pronounced, however, a sharp organizational change is likely, and the adult school may become a branch of the junior college. With the strong organizational loyalties and identifications that the adult administrators have developed, this type of change would not be readily accepted. The principals are firmly committed, after years of struggle to achieve a separate status, to the concept of a distinct administrative division for adult education.[23] They believe that in other units, such as the junior college, adult education becomes buried, consigned to a secondary or tertiary status.

The community college development has another type of impact upon

---

[21] *Ibid.*, p. 81.

[22] The Educational Policies Commission has long advocated community institutes as "the school system's agency of adult education." National Education Association, *Education for All American Youth*, p. 247. The President's Commission on Higher Education (1947) stated with emphasis, "The community college must be the center for the administration of a comprehensive adult education program." Bogue, *op. cit.*, p. 212. In arguing for the community college as the logical organization to assume the responsibility for adult education, leading California spokesmen (Sexson and Harbeson of Pasadena City College) make the point that "the organization of an evening high school or school of education unnecessarily complicates the machinery of public education." *Ibid.*, p. 209.

[23] *Report and Proceedings of the Montecito Workshop in Adult Education*, pp. 75–82.

the adult school that is not commonly perceived. This is an unanticipated consequence of competition. Competition between business firms heightens their adaptability to the marketplace. When it is threatened by competitors, a business firm will become more sensitive to its customers and their wants. The effect of competition among schools is much the same. The scramble for students and public support is intensified. As courses are transferred from one system to the other, or as students transfer because of more attractive offerings, the losing organization must attempt to plug the gaps left behind. Under such challenges to organizational welfare and personal position, the role of the administrator shifts toward the external duties of contacting new sources of clientele and bolstering existing relations to outside groups. Thus competition reënforces the trend toward an extreme service position. This particular effect of competition among school units seems unanticipated by school personnel.

These are some of the ways in which the community college movement becomes of major importance for the position and character of the adult school. Junior college representatives now openly suggest to the adult administrators that the time has come for the program to be transferred completely into the junior college, that it is naturally shifting from the high school level to the junior college.[34] As more junior college administrators learn the technique of community college organization and its advantages, the shift is likely to become more pronounced. Against this trend the adult school seeks to maintain its separate existence.

This chapter has reviewed two main sources of continuing insecurity for the adult school in the California public school system: the challenge to legitimacy from lay quarters, and the competition of the community college. The first causes insecurity by blocking the move of the adult school toward an accepted role; it tends to keep the program marginal. The community college contributes to insecurity by threatening to take over adult education within the local school system. This would not be a threat if the adult school were firmly established and accepted; it is vulnerable because of its marginality. Thus the challenge to legitimacy contributes to the second source of insecurity.

After this brief analysis of two current forces exerted upon the adult school, it may be well to restate one point: this study has *selectively* concentrated on the impact of a few pressures, from within and outside educational organizations, on a marginal school program, and

---

[34] See testimony of junior college administrators, *Partial Report of the Senate Interim Committee on Adult Education*, 1953, p. 313.

the way in which such pressures can shape the development of an institution. The presentation has been couched in terms of "pressure," "conflict," "dilemma," "problem," "tension." The pessimism conveyed by these terms is likely to be viewed as an undue accentuation of the negative. But it must be realized that this is a selective inquiry designed to emphasize the conditions and pressures that force organizational adaptations. From the beginning the research orientation guiding the analysis was a problem-conflict one, seeking sources of institutional change in the basic forces to which the adult school has had to adapt, regardless of the will of individual participants. Such underlying factors become apparent in persistent administrative problems and in situations of conflict not readily resolved. Hence the emphasis upon pressure and conflict. But while this is a selective analysis, it is believed that the participants and those well informed on school administration will recognize it as an accurate one. The emphasis upon attendance in this report, for example, is comparable to the emphasis it receives in administrative practice. Moreover, this report has indicated that such an emphasis is mainly a product of organizational conditions and processes, not a matter of "good" or "bad" motivation of individual administrators. There is little doubt that organizational marginality is a prime condition affecting the evolution of school programs and educational values. It is hoped that other inquiries will refine these points and further isolate the organizational developments that lead to predictable institutional trends in education.

CHAPTER VI

IMPLICATIONS FOR THEORY AND POLICY

THIS STUDY began with a brief description of evening-school activity in California schools before 1925. It then proceeded to the type of adult school that has developed over the last quarter of a century. In chapter ii an attempt was made to explain why this particular type of school has emerged. Many changing historical conditions were deliberately ignored so that the study might better highlight several fixed factors underlying the work of the adult school throughout an extended period.

Three conditions—marginal status, open-ended purpose, and a set of operating pressures—were the crucial aspects of the environment within which local administrators of adult schools made their decisions. These factors have been the immediate constants through which the effects of more removed and changing conditions have been funneled. The depression as a historical event affected the adult school principally through its main vulnerability, its marginal existence. Because of its peripheral status, the adult program suffered severely in the early 1930's and continued in a depressed state until it was rescued by a federal program set up to provide work relief for unemployed teachers.[1] World War II had its principal impact upon the adult school by changing the structure of community interests. In areas close to defense plants, the adult school was quick to take advantage of vocational training opportunities and other war service classes in 1941 and 1942. Organizational adjustment was not simply a patriotic endeavor; it was an expression of the adult school's orientation that it expanded rapidly in an area where there was an opportunity to give service. Many courses that had previously been stock-in-trade items became superfluous overnight and were jettisoned in the war-service-class adjustment.[2]

In interpreting the causes of institutional change, the evolution of programs and schools has been seen as emergent. An emergent evolution may be understood as a natural outcome of the conditions of a system of action, and as a trend relatively unguided by conscious planning. The

---

[1] See Emily M. Danton, "The Federal Emergency Adult Education Program," in D. Rowden, ed., *Handbook of Adult Education in the United States*, pp. 28–53. The decline in attendance size of the Los Angeles program after 1931–1932 (see table 4) was related to a decrease in program outlay from approximately $1,000,000 to $600,000. Program expenses did not reach the 1931–32 level again until 1939–40.

[2] The Los Angeles program added several thousand hours of war service classes in 1941–42, at the same time cutting back sharply in such categories as art crafts, dramatics, interior decorating, and millinery.

present institutional nature of these public schools has been determined by the succession of past short-run adaptations to environmental conditions. The foregoing analysis suggests that the defining modes of action of the adult school—those patterns by which it is known as an entity and perceived as a distinctive type of enterprise—have precipitated from practice as teachers and administrators have grappled with their own specific work problems. The analysis may be characterized, then, as a study of a natural institutional evolution. There seems to have been a minimum of over-all control and planned change. The implications of the study for sociological theory and educational policy lie mainly in the relation between organizational factors and unguided (unplanned, emergent) institutional modifications. In this concluding chapter, several of these connections will be traced further in order to infer the general conditions under which different types of institutional change take place. Since these inferences have meaning for educational practice, the points that seem most relevant to policy will be explicitly stated.

INSTITUTIONAL CHANGE

An institution may be conceived as essentially a configuration of behavioral patterns and related norms of conduct that has become well established and deeply valued.[3] Institutions have generally been considered in sociology as massive complexes of activities that serve the needs of a whole society. However, when properly conceptualized, institutions as behavioral complexes are seen to vary markedly in size. A meaningful configuration of behavioral patterns and related norms may be established in a relatively small part of a society. However delimited the set of established procedures, it may still be functioning as an institution, providing psychological satisfaction for those who have internalized the relevant standards. Participants in the situation feel "right" when they are conforming to the expected patterns. Then the approved patterns of action will also be fulfilling the social function of an institution, integrating individuals in social unities.[4] No lower limit.

---

[3] "Institution" is a broadly defined conception in sociology; since its intended empirical referents are configurational and complex, the concept has been ill defined for research purposes. At the same time, the phenomena referred to by the many definitions of institution seem so important for sociological theory that they cannot be ignored. For various definitions of "institution," see R. M. MacIver and Charles H. Page, *Society*, pp. 15–17; Talcott Parsons, *The Social System*, p. 39; John W. Bennett and Melvin M. Tumin, *Social Life*, pp. 166–169; Joyce O. Hertzler, *Society in Action*, pp. 191–193.

[4] On the psychological and social functions of institutions, see Parsons, *op. cit.*, pp. 36–45.

need be placed upon the size of a complex of behavioral standards for it to be conceived of as an institution.[8]

More importantly, institutions vary greatly in degree of fixity. In fact, institutional processes can hardly be studied without conceiving of institutionalization as a matter of degree. Some action patterns are much more firmly established, widely prized, and deeply valued than others, and it is usually the well-institutionalized configurations that are denoted by the customary definitions and descriptions in sociology. But the analysis of institutional development needs to be concerned with nascent and immature forms. In the latter connection, organizational action may be studied from the standpoint of institutionalization, since organizations tend to become institutions. In time a limited number of habitual types of action naturally emerge or are partially planned into being, with organizational personnel becoming attached to these habits as ends in themselves. Some members of the clientele, and perhaps of the general public, also become attached to the organization, valuing its procedures and therefore its existence. The organization as a whole may then become a valued symbol. Where such attachments have been formed, the organization is no longer a rationally ordered tool that may be dispensed with at will. For some, it is an institution.

When we speak of a "service institution" emerging within education, the term refers to the configuration of valued behavioral patterns and orientations that are centered on the cafeteria model of adult education. To the extent that this model is the dominant one in an adult school, the term "service institution" is an appropriate characterization of the school itself. This inquiry suggests that the service modes of conduct are indeed the dominant orientation of the California adult school, an emergent institution of considerable consequence. Of course, when the adult school is compared to the major institutions of education and of society at large, it appears as a weakly established and peripheral institution: the groups committed to this particular educational pattern are small; they have limited authority, power, and status; and the basic norms and patterns of action are still insecurely established. Within the smaller context of adult education itself, however, the service orientation is an important and perhaps the dominant tendency.

We shall next consider four characteristics of organization that generate unguided forms of institutional change.[9] These aspects of organization are generalized here, since they are potentially applicable to

---

[8] The lower limit is when "institution" becomes equal to "role"—the expectations upon behavior in one given social position. *Ibid.*, p. 39.

[9] One of the earliest treatments of institutions in American sociology, that of William Graham Sumner, stressed a distinction between *enacted* and *crescive* (un-

other contexts. They are: the nature of administrative purpose, the marginality of an organizational activity, the extent of centralization of authority, and the degree of professionalism among organizational personnel.

EFFECT OF ADMINISTRATIVE OBJECTIVES

Organizational goals have important bearing upon institutional evolution, for goals differ in the way they delimit individual behavior and organizational action. One of the first points noted in this study was that the stated objectives of adult education, such as economic efficiency, civic welfare, and cultural development, did not provide effective operational targets. Pronouncements on educational purpose have become a pseudo-mission, and this mainly because the goals of adult education agencies became so diffused after 1925 that they did not provide criteria relevant to decision-making. Rather, the emphasis in grass-roots administration has been upon purpose without limit. The adult school in California is a clear case of announced educational purposes fostering an *unplanned emergence of behavioral patterns out of day-to-day practice*. Open-ended goals cannot channel modifications in program and organization, but leave the type and direction of change to be determined by varying situations. Institutional development may thus be said to be highly situation-directed, and relatively little goal-directed.

A second finding in the study centered on the real purpose that has emerged. This is the omnibus purpose of service to the community, a conception much more widely voiced today than twenty-five years ago, and so elaborated that we may now speak of it as an ideology. This emergent purpose is seemingly a natural substitute for filling the vacuum left by the lack of program direction. The real purpose of administrators has tended to become that of building a service organization. However, this conception of purpose has a distinctive feature: it does not attempt to specify educational ends, but leaves program content to emerge in an undirected way. Purpose is centered on the creation of a certain relationship between a school and its clientele—the general service pattern wherein potential students present requests and the organization responds by adjusting its program. Using a psychological analogue, this relationship may be seen as a stimulus-response pattern, relatively unmediated by traditional program content. The response of the adult school to the stimuli-requests is not filtered through a concern with tradition, program continuity, and the proper ends of action.

---

enacted) institutions. More recent views have emphasized that all institutions have crescive elements, and that institutional development is mainly a matter of naturally emergent forms of behavior. See MacIver and Page, *loc. cit.*

Where the service conception is well established in administrative thought, the setting of program goals is no longer considered to be an important administrative activity. The adult school moves toward an extreme form of adaptive organization, becoming an agency that responds well to situational influences, but worries little about the implementation of educational ends.

This administrative conception has evolved out of practice over the last quarter of a century. When it is related to problems of organization, it may be seen as an adjustment of purpose to organizational needs: the survival and security of the adult schools in the context of open-ended goals, weak power and status, and the pressures of the enrollment economy. The discretion available to administrators within the broad limits of their manifest objectives has been used to strengthen the agencies with which the administrators are identified and upon which their own welfare depends. The short-run solutions to basic organizational problems were, obviously, to find clientele and build support. Thus the development of a diversified service program with little regard for content was a natural response of an insecure organization attempting to implement a broad conception of adult education.

Given the long-run democratization tendency in the public schools and the conditions specified in this report, a service type of organizational adaptation in the adult school would seem inevitable. The trend has been remarked upon elsewhere, but usually in a polemical context and with little attempt to treat it as a natural phenomenon within educational systems. At a general level it has been aptly described by Karl Mannheim as laissez-faire adult education, under the slogan "Give the people what they want," with little intervention by educators.[7] This case study has noted specific contextual determinants of a fairly extreme form of this trend. A general consequence of the trend has also been noted. Once the service orientation is well established in administration, the specific characteristics of the organization continue to emerge in an undirected way. The adult-school administrators become oriented away from planned programs; in addition, they can exercise little control.

The following generalizations may be made on the relationship of organizational goals to institutional development:

1. The more diffuse the goals of action agencies, the more an over-all institutional evolution will tend to be governed by emergent phenomena. Goal specificity, however, contributes to control over change. Thus the factor of specificity or generality of goals for firing-line agencies (not

---
[7] Karl Mannheim, *Freedom, Power, and Democratic Planning*, pp. 254–255.

for the field of effort in general) is an important variable in determining whether new rules and forms of procedure are to be developed in a controlled way.

2. The more diffuse the goals of action organizations, the more likely it is that an operationally relevant purpose will emerge from the pressures upon administration. The emergent purpose will be shaped by a second natural concern of executives, the survival and prosperity of the organizations with which leadership is identified.

3. An unguided evolution of school programs is favored when emphasis is placed upon the means of administration rather than upon educational ends. Program content will then tend to be uncontrolled, limited only by general types of administrative patterns. For an educational organization, the providing of a service program is not an educational goal; it is an administrative purpose centering on a broad type of relationship to clientele. The purpose of service is neutral in the choice of goals. The business of administrators becomes that of providing a diversified program, with its substance to be determined by the emergent trends of the future.

A further point needs to be made in order to clarify the relationship between goal generality on the one hand and organizational action and institutional evolution on the other. Chester I. Barnard has emphasized that a central function of executive action is "to formulate and define the purposes, objectives, ends, of the organization."[8] In practice this means taking the original ends of the entire organization and breaking them down into specific objectives. As we proceed from the top of an organization down to its lowest level, general purposes are broken down into subpurposes again and again, "resulting in closer and closer approximations to the concrete acts."[9] Diffuse goals, common at the highest reaches of large organizations, need not entail much unguided institutional change if there is an effective breakdown of purpose into subseries of goals for the smaller organizational units. The tendency outlined in the first generalization above must be considered with this limitation in mind.

In the educational activity described in this report, the original purposes of the adult education movement were so broadened after 1925 that it became synonymous with all adult learning; moreover, specialization of purpose was not carried out. The diffuse goals of higher levels of leadership have simply been transmitted down the organizational hierarchies to the smallest subunits of the adult education apparatus.

---
[8] Chester I. Barnard, *The Functions of the Executive*, p. 231.
[9] *Ibid.*

The emergent structure of the adult school has placed a number of obstacles in the way of an effective breakdown of purpose. First, the pressures of marginality and the enrollment economy force administrative action to be guided by situational imperatives and to be little affected by codes directly related to educational ends. Second, preprofessional administrative training has been inadequate, and there has been little opportunity to inculcate administrative codes *before* the principals face difficult problems of organization. Third, the conditions of work have not permitted the stabilization of a teaching force, and hence the transmission of specific purposes to lower personnel has been unduly complicated. Fourth, as a subunit of large organizations, the adult school has specialized not in subject matter but in serving a geographic area. In Los Angeles there have been a few important exceptions, such as the Americanization and Citizenship Center. Geographic specialization has naturally been called for by the spatial distribution of school plants and student populations, and has been favored by organizational pressures. Also, stable specialties within the separate schools, normally carried at other school levels by departments and permanent teachers, have not been feasible because of unstable staff and curriculum.

To understand the impact of organizational goals on a larger institutional evolution, then, we must consider also the nature of specialization of purpose.[10] Organizations have means-ends chains in which specific ends are the means to ultimate ones. The crucial question becomes whether the general purposes of a large organization can be split so as to leave the lower agencies with specific ends that are feasible in their setting. The environmental constraints upon adult education in the public schools have made the specification of purpose a difficult matter. The goal of servicing the community is a substitute for specialized educational targets, within an environment where laissez-faire programs develop naturally.

EFFECT OF MARGINAL STATUS

Peripheral programs within multiprogram organizations typically have low status and little power and, in consequence, are insecure. Worker education programs within trade unions and extension programs in universities, to take several examples, are plagued by the same difficulties that prevail within the public school framework: they are at the margin; they have low priority in the budget and frequently must pay

---

[10] For an informative discussion of specialization among organizational units, see Herbert A. Simon, D. W. Smithburg, and V. A. Thompson, *Public Administration*, chap. vii.

their own way; central administrators forget they exist as attention goes to basic functions; and, when retrenchments are in order, the unimportant programs are severely curtailed. Where the semiluxury program is handled by a separate unit within the larger structure, the agents of that unit find organizational existence itself somewhat precarious. This status affects almost everything the organization does, for no single attribute of organization colors thought and action more than a deep-seated insecurity. It affects employee morale, the incentives offered in recruitment of new employees, the feasibility of making long-range plans, the stability of budget, relationships with other departments, and the level of organization at which decisions are made. Above all, the need for adaptability is strengthened, in the sense of both conscious and unconscious adaptations that will help to stabilize the organization. In adjusting the purposes of an organization to its environment and vice versa, the attention of executives is necessarily centered on environmental situations. There is a greater mandate for adjustments made on other people's terms, and less likelihood that changes will be controlled from within.

Security is the prime prerequisite for responsibility in education, in the sense of consistent, goal-directed behavior.[11] Marginality, as a prime source of insecurity, tends to undercut the autonomy of administration, and to render decision-making more susceptible to external influences. Administrative action is then judged to be irresponsible, inconsistent in terms of goals, and overly responsive to immediate desires. This study has shown that the marginal status of adult education is likely to make administrators especially sensitive to the preferences of community groups, and oriented toward using the program for such ulterior motives as improving public relations for other school departments.

It follows that a peripheral status will shape administrative ideology, calling for doctrines that will strengthen the organization. Since marginality seeks adjustments beneficial to security here and now, it also demands an administrative ideology that will provide a morally satisfying rationale for these adjustments. In adult education, marginality has strengthened the need for a doctrine of service, or what might also be called a doctrine of immediate needs. The service doctrine currently in use may be viewed as a natural response to insecurity, for this ideology clearly sanctions the tendency to provide service to many groups within and outside the school system in return for their support.

[11] For an extended, general treatment of executive responsibility, see Barnard, *op. cit.*, chap. xvii.

A marginal position for an activity within larger organizations weakens the hand of its own work force in controlling its development. In its institutional consequences, this means that *organizational marginality will typically contribute to an unguided institutional evolution*.

EFFECT OF DECENTRALIZATION

Decentralization[12] works in the same direction as the previous two factors, permitting a greater degree of unplanned institutional development when compared to centralized administration. There is greater leeway for initiative and innovation by field administrators and subordinate personnel. The changes made are not likely to be uniform and will not be readily controlled from the top. In California this is evident at two levels within adult education. First, the autonomy of local districts within the state system weakens the control of the State Department of Education over field practices. Since local men have had the real program-setting authority, it is local decisions that have gradually brought about a service institution; the state's Bureau of Adult Education has been relatively powerless to affect the trend. This decentralization of authority conforms to the doctrine of local autonomy in American public education, which makes school systems highly adaptive to the interests of local communities. When educators or important interest groups feel that local programs are getting out of hand, however, they have a tendency to centralize authority in order to establish common patterns and to control undesirable practices. This is one of the objective effects of strong public attack upon a program—a heightening of pressure for central control. The normal situation, however, has been decentralization, with trends in the total state program emerging from the cumulative effect of thousands of local choices.

Second, when the autonomy of individual schools *within* local systems is strong, headquarters planning and coördination are less controlling. The principals of adult schools, while they are constrained by economy measures, usually have the discretion to adapt school programs to their clientele. Since the schools are geographically dispersed, principals and teachers must be allowed considerable leeway in making local adaptations without directions from headquarters. Then new classroom practices and other clientele innovations emerge continually as new possi-

---

[12] "Although individuals in organizations are not allowed complete discretion, organizations differ in the extent to which individuals or units within them may select their own premises of decision. When this is permitted to a relatively large extent, we say the organization is decentralized. When the opposite is true, we say that the organization is centralized." Simon, Smithburg, and Thompson, *op. cit.*, p. 367.

bilities appear. Where the administrative units are as widely dispersed as in the Los Angeles system, staff members at headquarters frequently can only guess what individual schools are doing. Decentralized discretion narrows the range within which central planning may control programs, and widens the range within which emergent phenomena will determine their evolution.

The recent state-wide controversy over the adult program (discussed in chapter v) provides an example of the effect of decentralized authority upon planned versus unplanned institutional changes. Some of the top administrators, who had been watching the trend in adult education since the equalization law was passed in 1947, saw that the adult-school administrators were living dangerously and that sooner or later the day of reckoning would come. Some administrators of adult education, including those in the state office, would have liked to control the drift of the program during the 1947–1952 period. But this was not possible within the existing structure of authority, and preaching did not have the effect upon decision-making that local pressures did, even when it came from respected figures. Good intentions without power to implement them could not stay the trend that brought the program under investigation. The state program could not be controlled by formally constituted authorities because the crucial decisions in program building are made by many highly decentralized agents.

This important aspect of formal organization has institutional consequences, one of which may be generalized as follows: the greater the degree of decentralized decision-making, the greater the leeway for an emergent institutional evolution.[13]

Effect of Professionalism

The professionalizing[14] of an occupation is a complex process that establishes codes of behavior which may be sanctioned from outside the occupation but are controlled mainly from within. Standards are set for entering the occupational group and for maintaining membership in good standing; in addition, a systematic effort is made to regulate

---

[13] For an excellent discussion of the effect of decentralization in business firms, one that has a different emphasis from that of the present discussion but similar implications, see James E. Worthy, "Organizational Structure and Employe Morale," *American Sociological Review*, 15 (April, 1950), pp. 169–179.

[14] Recent suggestive discussions of professionalism may be found in Gabriel A. Almond, *The American People and Foreign Policy*, pp. 236–237; Nelson N. Foote, "The Professionalization of Labor in Detroit," *American Journal of Sociology*, 58, no. 4 (January, 1953), pp. 371–380; Hertzler, *op. cit.*, pp. 204–205. For various conceptions of profession and a bibliography of the literature, see Morris L. Cogan, "Toward a Definition of Profession," *Harvard Educational Review*, 23 (1953), pp. 33–50.

future changes in the rules of conduct. Individual participants ideally must conform to professional standards. Formal codes are established, associations and committees are organized to uphold them, and formal and informal sanctions to be applied against the transgressor are elaborated. In its social meaning, therefore, professionalism is a complex mechanism of social control over individual behavior.

Even within education—an occupational field not thoroughly professionalized—various associations function as initiators and preservers of the professional attitude. The maintenance and the protection of teaching standards are also normal consequences of teacher communities. Where teachers are in close contact and identify closely with one another, adaptations in occupational behavior are controlled in part by the judgment of peers and therefore tend to be continuous with traditional ways. The same type of regulation and continuity of practice holds for administrative ranks. Even a modest degree of professional identification means some control of behavior by the peer group and its codes. If practices are to be modified, changes will be guided by professional research or expert assessment, and thus be controlled from within. In extreme cases, much rigidity may be produced. A profession may become so conservative that professionalism becomes dysfunctional for adaptation to changing social conditions. At a minimum, a move toward professionalizing an occupation has the effect upon institutional development of regulating conduct. Normative changes are guided by the work force directly concerned. This is surely a core aspect of the relationship between professionalism and institutional change.

An embryonic profession can be generated only on the basis of favorable work conditions. There must be a corps of full-time workers who are engaged in similar types of work and who are interested in their work as a permanent commitment. There must also be some degree of autonomy and a sense of performing a distinctive and valued activity. A potential profession cannot develop where there is no work basis for cultivating a sense of common identity. Where the minimal favorable conditions are present, teachers can begin to work actively for a higher professional status. The process of professionalization will, in turn, enhance the sense of commitment and common identification, and increase the autonomy of the work corps.

Among adult-school teachers, however, the work force is characterized by a low degree of professionalism. Indeed, the trend over the last quarter of a century has been away from the professionally trained day-school teacher and toward the part-time community teacher whose basic interests lie outside education. The adult-school teachers are not a distinct work group, since employment is temporary and part-time, and the teacher's status is uncertain. Conditions are unfavorable for the slow incubation of common standards. Innovations are not mediated through a community of peers and hence are not judged as a matter of professional practice. The absence of professionalism in the teaching force, because of the conditions of work and the highly responsive nature of the adult schools, leads to uncontrolled adaptations as teachers attempt to meet new demands thrust upon them. Control may be especially weak where teachers are dispersed over different hours of the day and days of the week, as well as being scattered in branch locations. In turn, principals and supervisors are hardly in a position to exercise control over a teaching force which is heterogeneous in interest, part-time in work commitment, and diffused over space and time. This is the major reason why it is difficult for headquarters personnel and school principals (and researchers) to know what is going on. It is difficult to grasp the totality of emergent changes in teaching practices and teacher-student relationships, and the type and magnitude of current changes remain partly unknown.

Several possible generalizations are indicated. First, professionalism has the function of increasing internal control over the evolution of patterns of behavior. Second, the teaching position in adult education in the public school is essentially nonprofessional. The result is a strengthening of the emergent evolution of procedures as over against controlled evolution. Third, a weakly professionalized teaching force will have weak standards. It is difficult to set and maintain standards without a full-time, permanently committed body of teachers.

These organizational conditions facilitate unguided institutional changes. They are potentially applicable to educational organizations other than adult schools and, at a higher level of generalization, to organizations in other fields. In the aggregate, they leave administrative action quite open-ended. The type of action that follows will be determined by specific situational factors and administrative responses thereto. In this case study, a complex of factors, the enrollment economy, proved to be the most important set of influences, providing the impulse for specific adaptations.

Over the last quarter of a century, adult schools have been faced with an increasingly differentiated, urban-oriented population that has more leisure time than ever before. To adapt to the general public, the schools obviously have had to contend with a heterogeneity of interests and with the changing content of adult leisure-time pursuits as the public fancy waxed and waned. So it might be said that the public literally forced the schools to evolve heterogeneous, flexible service programs. This explanation, however, does not account for the dynamics of organizational change.

Why did the adult schools of California, in fact, *choose* to adapt? To answer the question, we must understand the facilitating conditions specified above, and in addition, we must realize the impact upon administrative motivation of specific factors such as the mode of state aid. Organizations do not adjust automatically to a changing environment. Variations in adjustment patterns and in sharpness of response may be anticipated on the grounds of differences in organizational needs and interests. Or, similarities may be expected where basic factors are common to a number of organizations. The problem of institutional change in modern society is frequently a problem in organizational dynamics. Unless we utilize an organizational perspective, we miss important immediate causes of institutional change, or, of more consequence, we miss the intervening variables that may well be the most important determinants of change. This study has provided a concrete example: a specific relation between attendance and revenue which shapes the ready adjustment of California adult schools to the environment of public interests. Awareness of this relationship and its impact upon school administration is the heart of "knowing the score" in public school adult education in the state. But this factor must be seen in relation to other important determinants. The specific pressure for adaptation to a heterogeneous public has had considerable force *only* because it has operated under conditions that facilitated adaptation.

The enrollment economy as a generalizable factor must be subsumed at this time under the catch-all category of operating pressures. But even this broad category has utility, for it orients research toward the detailed, immediate pressures upon administration that would ordinarily escape a more general type of analysis. This is a particularly useful category to have in mind for research in education, since the impact of organizational pressures upon educational practices has not been well analyzed. The gap between educational research and the knowledge of the administrator is possibly greatest here, for research has tended to be highly segmental and focused on the technical problems of supervisory procedures, guidance programs, and efficient plant management. And as human relations research invades the schools, it usually focuses on problems of classroom participation and such areas as effective committee and conference technique. These are interesting and often important matters, but it is clear that small-group research is seldom oriented toward core problems of administration. The latter are likely to be investigated only when more general analyses are attempted. An institutional approach sees an entire school in relation to its internal and external environments, and thus is oriented toward the core activities of the school executive—the adjustment of an organization and its purposes to the pressures from within and outside the formal school apparatus.

The foregoing case study relates to a broad sociological generalization: emergent institutions are generated by the emergent needs and interests of social groups. In adult education these factors have been, on the one hand, the emergent, manifest interests of the adult population, and, on the other hand, the emergent needs and interests of the schools themselves. The dynamics of the emergence of a service institution within adult education cannot be understood without analyzing the needs of its organizational instruments.

INSTITUTIONAL INTEGRITY

This study permits a few observations on a difficult but important subject—the conditions necessary for maintaining institutional integrity,[15] in the sense of consistent lines of action that are related to long-run objectives. To attempt to judge integrity means to assess both the consistency of action and the rules by which the consistency is maintained. An individual may be consistent on various bases, as when his behavior is consistent in terms of maintaining his own job or protecting an organization. Personal integrity frequently must be judged on such grounds. But institutional integrity connotes the maintenance and protection of central values in a field of human effort.

There are numerous conditions of organizational decision-making that are likely to strain institutional integrity. The coexistence of several major contradictory codes is bound to cause much confusion over which values should be protected and what behavior is legitimate. Another important condition is insufficient administrative autonomy and organizational strength for warding off outside intervention. One condition usually contributes to the other. In chapter iv it was noted that the following explanations are frequently used in defending an adult course under attack: (1) the course produces such large enrollments that it more than pays for itself out of state funds and therefore local administrators should welcome its contribution; (2) the course should be encouraged rather than eliminated because it is good public relations for the school system; (3) the course should be continued be-

---

[15] Selznick has posed "the defense of institutional integrity" as one of the key tasks that leaders are called upon to perform. Philip Selznick, *Leadership in Administration*.

cause there is a heavy demand from the public for it; (4) the course is educationally valuable. The course may well have been educationally valuable, but the other arguments indicate that administrators are often swayed by extraneous "realistic" considerations. These intrusive factors stem from other codes, pertaining to the good of the organization or perhaps from an interpretation of democracy whereby "the customer is always right." When adult schools defend themselves on the first three grounds, however, they give the impression that their own program is not intrinsically worth while and that classes have been chosen on the basis of public relations, or income potential, or public pressure.

The use of the foregoing principles, of course, is often necessary in program defense, but unless their long-term effect upon integrity is understood and sufficient control is exercised, they have debilitating consequences. In effect, legitimacy is sought on grounds that are unstable as ideological props within school systems. The adult administrators find that "we give the people what they want" must usually be qualified by "if, of course, it is of educational value," simply because the latter is *the* core rationale for school programs. But this educational rationale will not hold for extreme "frill" courses that are hastily withdrawn when challenged, or for such distant subjects as the operation of canneries. In these it is only too evident that criteria of "educational value" play no important part.

Because of traditional expectations of surrounding groups, institutional integrity in adult education is strained by a basic contradiction: the traditional rules of the larger school system do not control what is done in the adult school; at the same time, the emergent codes of the adult school do not carry moral authority based on perceived educational value. Where the adult school attempts to be defined as both a service agency and a school, the conflict in orientation and justification tends to weaken institutional integrity. The rules of the adult school (e.g., class choice on the basis of demand) contradict the traditional premises of education and thus they appear as expedient administrative responses. Unless the ideology of service can be given a dependable moral footing, the adult school will be under continuing pressure to return to an educator model. It may be expected that formal standards will be increasingly elaborated by higher administrative levels, or by adult-school administrators under the press of criticism, in an effort to provide program channels and cut off the extremes of undesirable practice.

Institutional integrity normally depends upon the ability of the implementing organizations to maintain an approved consistency in practice and in ideology. This means that integrity is greatly determined by the degree to which experts control practice, as over against outside pressures. It may be suggested that institutional integrity is a function of (1) organizational self-definition, (2) autonomy from outside pressures, and (3) legitimacy of practice and ideology. The integrity of the adult school is under strain because of sharply divergent orientations, and confusing definitions of what should be done; administrative autonomy has been low, with practices determined by pressures from the community and from other school personnel; and service practices and ideologies are only partly accepted as proper for a school enterprise.

POLICY IMPLICATIONS

The foregoing discussions of institutional change and integrity have implications for policy. Decisions, of course, involve the values and preferences of educators, and choice rests with the responsible administrator. The role of the researcher in policy recommendations lies mainly in tracing the consequences of various lines of action, clarifying what has previously been known intuitively, perhaps, and, where possible, adding new information to the fund of knowledge with which administrators work. Several policy implications will be stated here in a tentative "if-then" form, followed by two specific recommendations pertaining to adult education alone.

CONTROL OF INSTITUTIONAL DEVELOPMENT

Action is delimited by goals and standards. If greater control over procedures in the adult school is desired, then administrators must set definite goals for each school over a certain period of time, give priorities and weightings to the different goals, formulate and maintain standards, and, particularly, instill professional codes in school personnel. These activities have one primary end in view: to give goals and standards a greater impact upon action. Goals and standards must be connected to specific administrative units. This is quite different from stating that adult-school educators must agree upon objectives and norms for the entire field—a fruitless quest in a complex society and especially in a field of endeavor in which no distinctive mission has been forthcoming. It is not necessary for all to agree upon the manifold objectives of adult education. It is necessary, however, that each action agency have a set of meaningful goals. Institutional control is purchased only at the price of a constant struggle with the task of choosing ends and shaping organizational structure and practice accordingly. This is a subjective, difficult business, a type of leadership activity that in the short run seems time-wasting and unproductive.

Conversely, if the control of institutional change is not considered desirable, and the school program is to be shaped by trends emerging from grass-roots practices, then goals and standards will be ignored. Such an orientation is commonly expressed as a willingness to tolerate experimental situations, with no imposing of predetermined schemes.

CONDITIONS FOR INTEGRITY OF PRACTICE

Extreme open-endedness in administrative orientation is obviously dangerous to organizational integrity. For *if* organizational responsibility is to be maintained, *then* key personnel need a minimal over-all pattern of what the organization desires to do and the proper rules for doing it. What basically matters is this: Have the leaders defined in their own minds what the organization in its totality should be? With some self-definition, their decisions can result in programs that lead toward the desired goal. Thus organizational integrity is, in part, dependent upon a sense of limits in organizational effort, a conception of what is relevant to the basic goals of the organization. This is directly related to adult education, where open-endedness of intent leaves administrators without a guiding self-definition.

The maintenance of integrity is likely to be difficult in schools making a service adaptation to environment. A strong other-directed orientation in administration, with its sensitivity to outside cues, means that consistent patterns can hardly be followed. At times planning is so minimal that it may be characterized as planning not to plan. A service program does not readily find limits; indeed, it is antithetical to the notion that a program should have limits. When service orientations are in full swing, no one knows what is proper or improper until it has been defined by the criticism of others. But the job of defining goals and standards can be ignored only at the risk of low integrity and an invitation to outside intervention. Those who do not know what they want will tend to become the tools of those who do.

Institutional integrity is related also to the degree of autonomy from outside groups. Many community groups feel that they have a right to participate in school decision-making. School administrators normally make a number of adjustments in order to maintain a workable equilibrium between the school and these surrounding social forces. Advisory committees are established, parent-teacher associations are utilized to interpret the school to the parent and to build grass-roots support, and representatives of interest groups are sometimes brought into curriculum committees. Such adjustments take place at all school levels; what is important is the type and extent of the participation of outsiders, for upon it there frequently turns the question of who is controlling the schools.

The problem of school autonomy has seemingly received little attention in programs where it is actually severe. In the adult schools, lay intervention has become the normal procedure. The autonomy of schoolmen is often not protected even in crucial areas of decision. The selection of teachers and courses seemingly requires professional determination. Yet lay groups frequently intervene decisively in these matters. At the extreme, outside groups may decide not only about teachers and courses but also about the location and scheduling of classes and the evaluation of student performance. In this way, institutional development may slowly and unconsciously be turned over to particularistic lay judgments, with decisions made not on the basis of what is good for the school but in accordance with the special interests of various groups. In the extreme case, the special competency of the professional administrator is denied, and his judgments are deemed to be no better than those of the client groups.

It seems clear that adult-education teachers and administrators will not be able to maintain a unified outlook and consistency in practice unless they seek and secure the degree of autonomy that will give them basic authority to determine what is done. A professional group need not be a closed, isolated body; but its ability to develop its province in consistent terms is dependent upon autonomy. Lacking this, institutional integrity will become impaired.

RECOMMENDATIONS

The foregoing policy implications have been necessarily general, and are intended to have relevance for policy formation throughout education. Here several specific recommendations pertain to the adult school alone. First, it is clear that the mode of financing adult education is crucial. Financing does not merely determine the over-all size of activity, but intervenes decisively in substantive matters. Perhaps the most practical implication of this study lies precisely in the analysis of appropriation-induced motivation.[16] When a state finances adult edu-

---

[16] The strategic role of appropriations has been observed elsewhere in administration, especially in the way in which congressional appropriations shape policy and administration in federal departments. See Charles M. Hardin, *The Politics of Agriculture*, pp. 159–164. That administrative motivation will commonly be shaped by the appropriations process seems reasonably apparent; yet the topic has been little explored and discussed.

cation on the basis of attendance, the pressure to increase student turnout is omnipresent in administration. In California it is virtually utopian *not* to expect average daily attendance to be the key concern in administration. This mandate is so strong in some schools that concern with the quality of work is actually detrimental to the welfare of the organization. Many adult administrators are well aware of this outcome of the state financial structure. Indeed, the advisability of shifting the basis for reimbursements to some other unit has been considered. But the move has not been openly sought because many adult administrators are still too insecure to risk the change. The present scheme is flexible: local administrators can increase their state aid by upping attendance. Other plans, such as financing on the basis of teaching hours or the matching of state and local support, are less flexible in this sense, and would entail a setback for some schools. Hence there is reluctance to abandon the present system for an uncertain change. But attendance will cease to be a central administrative concern only when it ceases to serve as the basis for financing. Educators need to consider seriously a change that would reward local effort and guarantee a minimum stability for adult-school programs, but that would at the same time permit program building to proceed on some basis other than student attendance.

A second recommendation relates to a division of work among organizations. It is commonly understood that as organizations mature they take on a set character. Like individuals, they become competent in certain lines of endeavor and incompetent in others. Established organizations, that is, institutions, do not take on new lines of activity easily, and there is virtually a dictum in public administration that a distinctively different program requires a new organization for effective implementation. This point has value for the present context in that it calls attention to the fact that there are limits on the range of competencies one organization may be expected to achieve. Where radically different competencies are desired, they may have to be organizationally separated.

In public school adult education there is considerable potential in a division of work between two types of units. The service program and the professionally dictated program are basically different types of effort; if both are deemed desirable, the establishment of separate subunits to perform them may well be the decisive step. This would be a minimal specialization of purpose. The adult school tends readily toward the service type, providing what might be called, at the extreme, a community-center facility. If the adult school evolved into a community center, school properties would be clearly identified as locations for all forms of adult participation. Community centers on school properties are eminently feasible, and such a development *within* adult education could be encouraged by means of programs earmarked as community-centered. Groups could obtain classes and facilities answering their diverse interests, regardless of the educational respectability of their demands. This could be an important contribution of the schools, highly functional for the adult population of a leisure-time society. Yet with the tradition of "proper" school behavior restricting them, the service-oriented schools cannot develop fully in this direction. In their present dual status, an open move toward a community-center role would endanger their claim to educational legitimacy and thereby render them more vulnerable. Community-center programs must now be smuggled in the back door and only partially developed.

The main stumbling block to adult schools becoming well-developed community centers lies in the source of income. An openly announced community-center program could not hope to be strongly supported by state funds, and hence would need much local support or would have to be virtually self-sustaining, with a system of fees for centers operated on a pay-as-you-go basis. Although a fee system is opposed by many adult-school administrators, it seems the main basis upon which school facilities can be developed as centers of adult recreation and leisure-time pursuits. At present there is no systematic community center development, and there is reason to believe that it is being stifled by a *sub rosa* existence within the schools.

The second type of program that seems desirable is the professionally set program, in line with the age-old ideals of adult education. The core rationale of adult education has long been that basic societal problems require a more enlightened population, and that this cannot be achieved by the training of the young alone. Indeed, adult-school educators emphasize that our social and political problems are so urgent that the development of a more intelligent population cannot wait upon the next generation. Yet the gap between ideals and actual practice has always been great.

Adult-school educators who are serious about putting their enlightenment ideals into practice can probably best attain their objective by setting aside organizational subunits for such a program. Schools, or distinctive parts of schools, established for this purpose would be educational in the traditional sense of the word. A sustained effort could be attempted in a limited number of curricula, organized for the progression of a small number of adults through sequences of articulated courses. Such agencies would obviously have attributes very different from those of service schools. They would require relatively small, stabilized staffs and would need to operate with small classes that could ignore attendance results. Units of this type could possibly experiment with week-end schools, or other forms of concentrated participation, similar to the current folk university in English adult education.[17] A school system making this major division of work between organizations would have a large community-center program and a relatively small educator one. Different types of personnel would need to be recruited and distinctive orientations developed in each. In this way, organizations highly competent in the two main lines of endeavor could mature. This separation of purposes would strengthen the integrity of adult education agencies, improve their competencies, and reduce the stress of incompatible demands. On the one hand, the fully evolved service schools would not need to claim a traditional educational role; on the other hand, curriculum-oriented programs would not have to be adjusted from month to month to changing clientele interests. Given the natural drift toward service programs, it would be the "imposed" type of program that would need special protection. If the public schools want adult programs that are not content with the educational *status quo*, they need specific organizations strongly oriented toward this type of effort. It seems likely that community centers and folk schools will both thrive within adult education when they are clearly perceived as different types of adult education effort and are given separate organizational status.

[17] See Guy Hunter, *Residential Colleges*. The British residential schools for adults developed after World War II, and are somewhat of an attempt to emulate the folk high schools of Denmark and Sweden, "where somehow a quite considerable proportion of ordinary citizens seemed both to want and to be able to take no less than five or six months of residential education in humane subjects and particularly in the literature, history, and religion of their own country." *Ibid.*, p. 17.

APPENDIXES

Appendix I
METHODOLOGY OF THE RESEARCH

The field research for this study was carried out between July, 1952, and August, 1953, as a one-man endeavor. Since school administrators are frequently approached by educational researchers, entry into the Los Angeles school system was readily arranged. The initial procedure was to become immersed in the organization —as fully as it is possible for a nonparticipant in a limited time—in order to acquire maximum insight on both formal and informal aspects of organization. This can best be accomplished by observation, interviewing, and documentary analysis.[1]

Informal observation included routine attendance at board of education meetings, where an observer learns little about a school organization until he has mastered the cues for interpreting what is being said, or left undone; and attendance at local and state meetings of adult education personnel. The routine operation of headquarters offices, the functioning of adult school offices and classrooms, and the overt interaction between various types of personnel were also observed. Such informal observation of behavior over an extended period gives a sense of the concrete organization in action. In this case it was indispensable for becoming personally acquainted with the wide range of classes in the schools and the variety of patterns of classroom adjustment.

Informal interviewing was of greater value, however, especially for attaining knowledge of administrative problems. From the beginning of the research, much time was given to interviews with administrators and supervisors in and outside the adult units in the Los Angeles system, and with administrators in surrounding school systems; informal discussions were held also with representatives of interest groups who took a stand on adult education. Several subjects were explored at each interview, lasting one to two hours, but the conversation was allowed to drift according to the interests of the respondent. Thus the subject matter for the interviews shifted from day to day. This flexible procedure is highly useful in exploration, since it adapts to the real problems of respondents rather than having them answer a fixed set of questions. In this way, definitions of the situation emerge that constitute an accumulative index of administrative orientation. The materials gathered in this informal manner were controlled indirectly by crosschecking answers of different respondents and particularly by checking interview responses against the written record.

Qualitative documentary analysis provided the greatest amount of reliable information on various organizational decisions. Organizational records are, of course, actually a scrambled organizational history. Persistent problems, the determinants of policy, and important decisions get down on paper, at least in partial form. The researcher's task is to use all available clues to unscramble the record. Organizational documents, public and private, were perused for several months in order to gain insight into the problems and thought categories of school administrators. Attention was guided partly by problem areas considered to be potentially im-

---

[1] For recent discussions of methodology that are somewhat relevant to institutional analysis, see Robert K. Merton *et al.*, eds., *Reader in Bureaucracy*, Part VIII, "Field Methods for the Study of Bureaucracy"; Paul F. Lazarsfeld and Allen H. Barton, "Qualitative Measurement in the Social Sciences," in Daniel Lerner and Harold D. Lasswell, eds., *The Policy Sciences;* and Alvin W. Gouldner, *Patterns of Industrial Bureaucracy*, Appendix, "Field Work Procedures—The Social Organization of a Student Research Team."

portant, such as the criteria for the selection of teachers, the nature of the adult school's relationship to students and community groups, and its relations to other segments of the school system. But these broad areas of exploration did not determine the ultimate focus of the research. Following the initial undirected reading of documents, attention became more selective: at first in order to follow out leads provided in interviews, and later to seek detailed information on the factors isolated as most important.

Despite the initial open-endedness of the analytical framework, the research problem still had to undergo a major revision. This was a direct result of the informal methodology, since the written record suggested a central but unanticipated aspect of organizational action. Initially it had been decided to ignore the routine business side of the adult program in order to concentrate on the social factors in the evolution of an educational program. This defined economic matters to be mostly outside the scope of the study. But from the interviews, some previous studies, and particularly the organizational records, the influence of the enrollment economy in shaping adult education units emerged. Concern with attendance was seldom stated explicitly, but it soon became apparent that it lay beneath the surface in all kinds of organizational problems. The structure of the teaching force could not be understood without seeing the influence of the enrollment economy. The research had to be redirected to center upon what seemed an essentially unsociological topic, for attendance is a prosaic concern, not calculated to excite social scientists. But an institutional analysis that did not take enrollment pressures into account would have been false, or superficial at best.

The level of analysis also had to be shifted, or, more accurately, an attack made on an additional level. In order to find the determinants of organizational pressures, the problem of program building had to be considered not only on the local level but in terms of state-wide conditions. In this way the project became more than a study of the adult school in Los Angeles. Hence the informal techniques of the field research led to a major unanticipated finding and to a shift in levels of analysis.

After eight months of research it was possible to arrive at a tentative explanation of an institutional development. The research then centered on gathering evidence for or against this general hypothesis. In particular, information was sought on the systematic effects of state legislation and the underlying meaning of the state-wide controversies over adult education. Thus the work became progressively narrowed. The last few months of inquiry were given mainly to devising and administering the mail questionnaire by which additional systematic information on adult-school teachers was gathered.

Organizational research is frequently productive of administrative anxiety,[3] since research may be somewhat disturbing to an organization or is perceived as potentially threatening. This likelihood increases when organizations are insecure, and particularly when they are undergoing the scrutiny of higher authorities. Then, more than usual, the organizational guard must be up. By coincidence the field research was done at a time when the adult school was under stress because of attack from the state legislature. This had a major advantage for the research in that the organization could be studied while it was under tension, and the responses called out by the controversy could be observed. At the same time, however, a crisis has

---

[3] Robin M. Williams, Jr., "Application of Research to Practice in Inter-Group Relations," *American Sociological Review*, 18 (February, 1953), pp. 78–83.

the disadvantage of increasing anxiety about research done on internal aspects of organization. Some principals had warned their teachers against talking freely with outsiders about adult-school business. Establishing the legitimacy of the research thus became a special problem. Several letters of introduction from sources within and outside the school system were used to identify the work as an academic project, and little difficulty was encountered in making personal contacts. Only two administrators refused, and their refusals were not prompted by anxiety. However, among those interviewed, more caution than usual may have been exercised. Some of the interviews stayed on very safe ground.

Ordinarily, impersonal, formal research techniques would be considered less disturbing than informal ones that permit personal probing. But in a context productive of anxiety, impersonal techniques may be received unfavorably. They are not mediated by face-to-face contact, and the cold relationship between subject and researcher leaves less opportunity for explanation. Personal contact, even if probing in nature, is more reassuring. The researcher can be identified and assessed more readily. Also, the analyst touches the organization one person at a time, and any impact he may have is spread over time and thereby muted. The formal techniques of systematic interview, observation, and questionnaire, however, announce that research is going on.

In this study the formal technique of mailing questionnaires to one-third of the teachers produced concern among the teachers and was considered unnecessarily provocative by the administrators. Rapport had to be repaired, and the point made anew that the researcher was not connected with any interest group or legislative committee. Administrators do not like to have sensitive matters probed and possibly agitated by research, while researchers do not want their work suppressed by administrative viewpoints when the two conflict. The working out of such problems requires good will between administrators and analysts, and, in situations of organizational struggle, forbearance on the part of the organization. Where rapport is sustained, as it was in this project, it is due mainly to the generosity of those on the receiving end of the study.

An institutional study involves a search for the significant factors in a complex situation of social action. A strong point in such studies is their relevance to real problems and to significant aspects of behavior in a given situation. The orientations fruitful in such a search, however, naturally favor an emphasis upon discovery and less emphasis on close, immediate validation of research results. Moreover, the use of formal techniques is limited if the inquiry takes place within organizations, and the possibilities of clear and direct proof are thereby narrowed. For example, validating the central theme of this study is a matter of a number of indirect and partial indicators, which taken together suggest that the interpretation is a true one. As a fairly complex interpretation of institutional change, it is provable only in indirect, partial ways, regardless of what techniques are used. The lack of immediate validation is defensible in that the ultimate validity of all research rests not in the tests of significance of the moment but upon whether the findings hang together with findings from other studies to produce a theoretical structure. But, in the short run, institutional analyses must be judged methodologically weak in providing opportunity for others to assess their validity.

This weakness may well be remedied in the future through improvements in technique. The greatest improvement can be obtained immediately within the confines of single studies, however, through longer periods of field work. Case studies lasting several years permit greater leeway in shifting from a context of discovery to one of validation as a project develops. Then an interpretation achieved in the earlier stages of research can be better tested by data gathered in systematic ways.

APPENDIX II

QUESTIONNAIRE ON TEACHING STAFF

A four-page questionnaire was mailed to 337 adult-school teachers in June, 1953, in order to gather additional data on characteristics and identifications of the teaching staff. This was a one-third sample of the total teaching force, drawn by taking every third name from an alphabetical file; 181, or 54 per cent, of the questionnaires were returned. The respondents thus constitute a self-selected sample that totals more than one-sixth of the total force. All the questions are reproduced in their original order. In addition to the information presented in chapter iii, analysis of data from the questionnaire may be found in Appendixes III and IV.

MAIL QUESTIONNAIRE

1. How many years have you taught in adult education? ....
   (Years)
2. What credential do you have?   *Check one*
   (1) Adult Education Credential.................................. ....
   (2) Vocational Type D Credential................................ ....
   (3) General Secondary Credential................................ ....
   (4) Special Secondary Credential................................ ....
   (5) Other (specify)... ....
3. Do you know what your "tenure" status is? Yes .... No ....
   If "yes": what is it?
   (1) Substitute status... ....   (3) Probationary status.... ....
   (2) Temporary status.. ....   (4) Permanent status...... ....
4. How many hours this past school year would you estimate that principals and/or supervisors have spent with you on your classes? (Sept., 1952–June, 1953)
   Check one
   (1) none................. ....
   (2) 1–5 hours........... ....
   (3) 6–10 hours.......... ....
   (4) 11–20 hours......... ....
   (5) over 20 hours....... ....
5. Whom do you consider the most important judge of your teaching?
   Check one
   (1) the principal......... ....
   (2) other teachers........ ....
   (3) the students......... ....
   (4) myself............... ....
   (5) supervisors.......... ....
   (6) none of the above.... ....   If (6), who?.....................
6. How much longer do you *want* to remain in adult-school teaching?
   Check one   *Check one*
   (1) no more............. ....   (4) 5–9 more years....... ....
   (2) 1–2 more years...... ....   (5) 10 years or more..... ....
   (3) 3–4 more years...... ....   (6) Don't know.......... ....

7. Which of the following statements is closest to your assessment of the adult-school program?

   Check one
   (1) The program should have a *greater* variety of courses......... ....
   (2) The program should remain about as varied *as it is now*....... ....
   (3) The program should have *less* variety of courses............. ....

8. What is the nature of your contact with other adult-school teachers?

   Check one
   (1) I am *very close* to other adult-school teachers................ ....
   (2) I have *some contact* with the other teachers................... ....
   (3) I have *little or no contact* with the other teachers............. ....

9. Are you concerned with the opinion in which you are held by the other adult-school teachers?

   Check one
   (1) I consider their opinion *quite important*..................... ....
   (2) I am *mildly concerned* about their opinion.................... ....
   (3) I have *little or no concern* about their opinion................ ....

10. During the past year, have you discussed the content of the adult education program with other adult-school teachers?

    Check one
    (1) I have discussed it *numerous times* with other teachers........ ....
    (2) I have discussed it *a few times* with other teachers............ ....
    (3) I have *not discussed* it with the other teachers................ ....

11. Is it important to you whether or not the adult-school teachers spend more time together than they do now?

    Check one
    (1) I consider it *quite important*................................ ....
    (2) I consider it to be of *some importance*....................... ....
    (3) I consider it of *little or no importance*...................... ....

12. From your experience, would you say that the adult schools have definite teaching standards?

    Check one
    (1) The adult schools have *definite* teaching standards............ ....
    (2) The adult schools have *vague* teaching standards............. ....
    (3) The adult schools have *no* discernible teaching standards..... ....

13. Do you feel that, in general, courses should be added to the program according to the demand for them?

    Check one
    (1) Courses should *always* be added according to demand......... ....
    (2) Courses should *sometimes* be added according to demand...... ....
    (3) Courses should *not* be added according to demand............ ....

14. Do you feel that a teacher should be dismissed when his classes fall below a certain minimum size?

    Check one
    (1) I feel that the teacher *should be dismissed*..................... ....

(2) I feel that other factors should be considered and the teacher *frequently kept on*.. ....
(3) I feel that class size should not be important, and the teacher *definitely kept on*.. ....

15. In your opinion, does the policy of discontinuing small classes have a beneficial or a harmful effect on teaching?

    Check one

    (1) It has a *beneficial* effect.. ....
    (2) It doesn't have much effect either way....................... ....
    (3) It has a *harmful* effect.. ....

16. From your experience, what is your estimate of the job that the adult-school principals are doing in building an adult education program?

    Check one

    (1) The principals are doing a *good* job of building the program.... ....
    (2) The principals are doing a *fair* job of it....................... ....
    (3) The principals are doing a *poor* job of building the program ... .

17. What would you consider to be your primary motive for teaching in the adult schools?

    Check one

    (1) The satisfaction derived from teaching adults ....
    (2) The income from the work................................... ....
    (3) The work conditions are better than in teaching lower grades . ...
    (4) An opportunity to further myself in the school system......... ....
    (5) An opportunity to further myself outside the school system ... .
    (6) Some other reason (specify).................................. ....

18. For EACH CLASS you teach in the adult schools, please fill in the following: (for the period since Feb., 1953; if more than six classes, please continue on the back of this sheet)

Class	Name of Class	Hours per Week	No. of Weeks	Student Enrollment	Location
No. 1					
No. 2					
No. 3					
No. 4					
No. 5					
No. 6					

Total hours per week ....

19. To the best of your knowledge, what was the main "source" of each class?

Class	Outside request (petition, etc.)	Your own idea	Check one for each class Principal's idea	Hq's idea	Other (specify)	Don't know
No. 1	( )	( )	( )	( )	( )	( )
No. 2	( )	( )	( )	( )	( )	( )
No. 3	( )	( )	( )	( )	( )	( )
No. 4	( )	( )	( )	( )	( )	( )
No. 5	( )	( )	( )	( )	( )	( )
No. 6	( )	( )	( )	( )	( )	( )

20. If some of your classes were requested by, or otherwise connected with, an outside group or organization, please fill in the following:

Class	Name of the Group	Class	Name of the Group
No. 1		No. 4	
No. 2		No. 5	
No. 3		No. 6	

BACKGROUND CHARACTERISTICS

1. What is your age?....... ....
2. Sex: Male............ ....
   Female.......... ....
3. What is your marital status?
   Check one
   (1) Single............... ....
   (2) Married............. ....
   (3) Widowed, Separated, or Divorced.......... ....
4. Do you have children? Yes............
   No............
   If "yes": how many?.... ....
   What are their ages?
   ....
5. What level of *formal* education have you completed?
   Check one   *Check one*
   (1) Eighth-grade graduation............... ....
   (2) High school diploma ....
   (3) Associate of Arts Degree............. ....
   (4) Bachelor's Degree... ....
   (5) Master's Degree..... ....
   (6) Doctor's Degree..... ....
6. What is your religious affiliation, if any?
   Check one   *Check one*
   (1) Catholic............. ....
   (2) Jewish.............. ....
   (3) Protestant........... ....
   (4) Other.............. ....
   (5) None.............. ....

7. In what outside clubs or organisations (other than work) do you take an active part? (If none, please write none).
   (1) .... (3) ....
   (2) .... (4) ....

8. What employment do you have other than adult teaching?
   Check one
   (1) *No work other than adult teaching*............................... ....
   (2) *Housewife*.. ....
   (3) *Full-time day-school* teaching................................. ....
      (main subject:..)
   (4) *Full-time* position outside of teaching......................... ....
   (5) *Part-time* position outside of teaching......................... ....
     For *(4) or (5)*:
      Title of job: ....
      Type of industry: ....
      Hours per week: ....

9. What was your income from adult teaching during the past twelve months?

	Check one		*Check one*
(1) Under $500...........	....	(6) $2,500–$2,999.........	....
(2) $500–$999............	....	(7) $3,000–$3,499.........	....
(3) $1,000–$1,499........	....	(8) $3,500–$3,999.........	....
(4) $1,500–$1,999........	....	(9) $4,000 and over......	....
(5) $2,000–$2,499........	....		

10. What was the approximate income of your family unit, from all sources, during the past twelve months?

	Check one		*Check one*
(1) Under $3,000.........	....	(5) $6,000–$6,999.........	....
(2) $3,000–$3,999........	....	(6) $7,000–$7,999.........	....
(3) $4,000–$4,999........	....	(7) $8,000 and over......	....
(4) $5,000–$5,999........	....		

Appendix III

SOCIOECONOMIC CHARACTERISTICS OF RESPONDENTS TO QUESTIONNAIRE

Men and women teachers differ considerably in age, the men being relatively young and the women relatively old. One-half of the men are under forty, as compared to less than one-fifth of the women (table A).

The sexes differ also in marital status. Over four-fifths of the men are married, as compared to less than one-half of the women. Over one-fourth of the women are widowed, separated, or divorced (table B).

Less than 3 per cent of the men reported adult teaching as their only occupation, while more than half of the women have this occupational status (table C).

TABLE A
Age and Sex

Age	Male		Female		Total	
	No.	Per cent	No.	Per cent	No.	Per cent
20–29	13	11.6	3	4.9	16	9.3
30–39	45	40.2	8	13.1	53	30.6
40–49	32	28.6	21	34.4	53	30.6
50–59	15	13.4	22	36.1	37	21.4
60 and over	7	6.2	7	11.5	14	8.1
No answer	2	....	6	....	8	....
Total	114 (63.0)	100.0	67 (37.0)	100.0	181 (100.0)	100.0

TABLE B
Marital Status and Sex

Marital status	Male		Female		Total	
	No.	Per cent	No.	Per cent	No.	Per cent
Single	14	12.4	17	25.4	31	17.2
Married	96	84.9	31	46.3	127	70.6
Widowed, separated or divorced	3	2.7	19	28.3	22	12.2
No answer	1	....	0	....	1	....
Total	114	100.0	67	100.0	181	100.0

TABLE C
Primary Occupation and Sex

Occupation	Male		Female		Total	
	No.	Per cent	No.	Per cent	No.	Per cent
Regular day teaching	72	63.2	20	29.9	92	50.8
Full or part-time outside job	39	34.2	12	17.9	51	28.2
Adult teaching only	3	2.6	35	52.2	38	21.0
Total	114	100.0	67	100.0	181	100.0

Education	No.	Per cent
Eighth grade	3	1.7
High school diploma	15	8.4
Associate of Arts Degree	16	9.0
Bachelor's Degree	65	36.5
Master's Degree	71	39.9
Doctor's Degree	8	4.5
No answer	3	....
Total	181	100.0

Religion	No.	Per cent
Catholic	19	11.0
Jewish	11	6.4
Protestant	122	70.5
Other	4	2.3
None	17	9.8
No answer	8	....
Total	181	100.0

In 1952–53 only about 10 per cent of the teachers made over $4,000, the equivalent of a full-time salary, from their adult teaching alone.

Income	No.	Per cent
Under $1,000	70	40.0
$1,000–$1,999	65	37.1
$2,000–$2,999	13	7.4
$3,000–$3,999	9	5.2
$4,000 and over	18	10.3
No answer	6	....
Total	181	100.0

In income from all sources, however, four out of five respondents have a family income of over $5,000 and fall into middle-income brackets. One-fifth are in the "$8,000 and over" category.

Income	No.	Per cent
Under $4,000	12	7.2
$4,000–$4,999	23	13.9
$5,000–$5,999	36	21.7
$6,000–$6,999	32	19.3
$7,000–$7,999	26	15.6
$8,000 and over	37	22.3
No answer	15	....
Total	181	100.0

Appendix IV
ADDITIONAL STATISTICAL INFORMATION ON QUESTIONNAIRE

1. "How many years have you taught in adult education?"

Appendix III shows a male-female differential in age, marital status, and occupation. Table D indicates that teachers with long experience in adult education are predominantly women.

2. "What credential do you have?"

Women teachers are more likely to have an adult education credential or a special secondary and less likely to have a general secondary than men teachers (table E).

TABLE D
Teaching Experience and Sex

No. of years	Male		Female		Total	
	No.	Per cent	No.	Per cent	No.	Per cent
0–4	64	60.4	16	26.7	80	48.2
5–9	26	24.5	15	25.0	41	24.7
10–14	9	8.5	8	13.3	17	10.3
15–19	5	4.7	7	11.7	12	7.2
20 and over	2	1.9	14	23.3	16	9.6
No answer	8	....	7	....	15	....
Total	114	100.0	67	100.0	181	100.0

TABLE E
Teaching Credential and Sex

Credential	Male		Female		Total	
	No.	Per cent	No.	Per cent	No.	Per cent
Adult Education	22	19.3	18	26.9	40	22.1
Vocational Type D	12	10.5	1	1.5	13	7.2
General Secondary	69	60.5	26	38.8	95	52.5
Special Secondary	9	7.9	22	32.8	31	17.1
Other: Vocational Type A	2	1.8	0	....	2	1.1
Total	114	100.0	67	100.0	181	100.0

3. "Do you know what your 'tenure' status is?"

Regular day teachers have tenure in their day positions. Of the remaining adult teachers, less than three-fourths indicate that they know what their teacher status is. Of those who believe they know, four out of five believe they have permanent status. There is possibly much misperception among the teachers on this point since their permanency is usually in doubt. This question was resented by some of the administrators, since it touched upon a delicate aspect of the teacher-school employment relation.

Those other than regular day teachers answered as follows:

	No.	Per cent
Yes	63	72.4
No	24	27.6
No answer	2	....
Total	89	100.0

Of those who answered "yes": believe status to be

	No.	Per cent
Substitute status	2	3.3
Temporary status	5	8.2
Probationary status	4	6.5
Permanent status	50	82.0
No answer	2	....
Total	63	100.0

4. "How many hours this past school year would you estimate that principals and/or supervisors have spent with you on your classes?" (Sept., 1952–June, 1953)

	No.	Per cent
None	58	32.6
1–5 hours	92	51.7
6–10 hours	18	10.1
11–20 hours	4	2.2
Over 20 hours	6	3.4
No answer	3	....
Total	181	100.0

5. "Whom do you consider the most important judge of your teaching?"

	No.	Per cent
The principal	10	5.7
Other teachers	1	0.6
The students	144	82.8
Myself	16	9.2
Supervisors	3	1.7
No answer or multiple answers	7	....
Total	181	100.0

6. "How much longer do you *want* to remain in adult-school teaching?"

	No.	Per cent
No more	11	6.3
1-2 more years	20	11.4
3-4 more years	17	9.6
5-9 more years	18	10.2
10 years or more	63	35.8
Don't know	47	26.7
No answer	5	....
Total	181	100.0

16. "From your experience, what is your estimate of the job that the adult-school principals are doing in building an adult education program?"

	No.	Per cent
Principals doing a good job	122	70.5
Principals doing a fair job	41	23.7
Principals doing a poor job	10	5.8
No answer	8	....
Total	181	100.0

17. "What would you consider to be your primary motive for teaching in the adult schools?"

In self-assessment, one-half of the respondents reported satisfaction from the work and one-third indicated income as a motive. For the regular day teachers alone, income was the dominant factor (table F).

Those who report satisfaction as a primary motive are more closely identified with the organization than those who report income (table G). (The identification score is based on a composite score, as reported in chap. iii.)

TABLE F
ASSESSMENT OF MOTIVE FOR TEACHING

Motive	All respondents		Regular day teachers only	
	No.	Per cent	No.	Per cent
Satisfaction derived from teaching adults	77	50.6	26	33.3
Income from the work	54	35.5	47	60.3
Work conditions better than in teaching lower grades	2	1.3	0	....
Opportunity to further myself in school system	1	0.7	1	1.3
Opportunity to further myself outside school system	1	0.7	0	....
Some other reason	17	11.2	4	5.1
Multiple answer or no answer	29	....	14	....
Total	181	100.0	92	100.0

TABLE G
IDENTIFICATION SCORE AND MOTIVE

Identification score	Satisfaction		Income	
	No.	Per cent	No.	Per cent
High (4–6).........	20	27.0	3	5.6
Medium (7–9).......	37	50.0	27	50.0
Low (10–12)........	17	23.0	24	44.4
Total............	74	100.0	54	100.0

APPENDIX V

PRELIMINARY REGISTRATION FORM
LOS ANGELES CITY SCHOOL DISTRICT
PETITION AND PRELIMINARY REGISTRATION FOR EVENING ADULT CLASS

TO:.., Principal

....Evening High School

For the establishment of any of the evening adult courses, at least forty (40) bona fide applicants must register. Art Crafts, Consumer Buying, Parent Education, Dressmaking, Millinery, Home Nursing, Chorus, Piano and Voice, Spanish, and other subjects are available.

Day preferred:..........................

Subject requested: .... Hours preferred:..........................

I realize that regular attendance and strict attention to class work will be necessary to carry on the work of this course in a creditable manner. In signing this petition I hereby pledge myself to attend punctually all of the sessions of this class unless prevented from doing so by illness or other circumstances beyond my control.

| NAME | ADDRESS | TELEPHONE |

1. ....

2. ....

3. ....

4. ....

- -

40. ....

APPENDIX VI

ADULT SCHOOL CLASS SCHEDULES

HOLLYWOOD ADULT SCHOOL, 1952-53
(Largest Adult School in Los Angeles)

SCHEDULE OF EVENING CLASSES

Subject	Days	Hours
Advertising Illustration	M	7:00-10:00
Algebra—Elementary and Advanced	MW	7:00- 9:00
Bookkeeping and Accounting—Beginning	MWF	7:00- 9:30
Bookkeeping and Accounting—Advanced	TuTh	7:00- 9:30
Chemistry—General	TuTh	7:00-10:00
Chemistry—Industrial	TuTh	7:00-10:00
Choral Production I	Tu	7:00-10:00
Choral Production II	Th	7:00-10:00
Citizenship (3 classes)	TuTh	7:00- 9:00
Civics	M	6:30- 9:30
Clothing Construction I	M	6:30- 9:30
	W	6:30- 9:30
Clothing Construction II	Tu	6:30- 9:30
	Th	6:30- 9:30
Counseling and Guidance	MTuWThF	6:30- 9:30
Current History—The World Today	Tu	7:00-10:00
Drafting—Architectural and Mechanical	TuTh	7:00-10:00
Driver Education	M	7:00- 9:30
Economics and Investments	F	7:00- 9:30
English I—Correct Speech, Usage	TuTh	7:00- 9:30
English II—Composition, Syntax, and Punctuation	MW	6:30- 8:00
English III—American Literature	MW	8:00- 9:30
English IV—English Literature and Vocabulary Building	F	6:30- 9:30
English V—Commercial Writing	Tu	7:00-10:00
English VI—Commercial Writing	W	7:00-10:00
English VII—Writing for Radio and Television	M	7:00-10:00
English VIII—Writing for Radio and Television	W	7:00-10:00
English IX—Professional Study and Voice Training	TuTh	6:30- 8:00
English X—Radio Acting Technique	TuTh	8:00-10:00
English XI—Advanced Radio and Television Acting	WF	7:00-10:00
English XII—Verse Writing	M	6:30- 9:30
English XIII—Public Speaking	MW	7:00- 9:30
English XIV—Speech Problems Correction	F	7:00- 9:00
English XV—Lip Reading	MW	7:00- 9:00
English for Foreign Born I	MWF	6:30- 9:30
English for Foreign Born II	MWF	6:30- 9:30
English for Foreign Born III	TuTh	6:30- 9:30
English for Foreign Born IV	TuTh	6:30- 9:30
101 Great Books	M	7:30- 9:30
French I	MW	7:30- 9:30

Subject	Days	Hours
French II and III	TuTh	7:00- 9:00
Freehand Drawing	MW	7:00-10:00
Geology and Mineralogy	TuTh	7:00-10:00
Geometry—Plane	MW	7:00- 9:00
Gerontology	M	7:30- 9:30
Home Decoration I—Copper and Leather	TuTh	7:00-10:00
Home Decoration II—Ceramics	MTuWThF	7:00-10:00
Home Decoration IV—Lampshades	Tu	7:00-10:00
Horticulture Judging II	F	7:00-10:00
Instruments—Stringed	F	7:00-10:00
Interior Decoration I	M	7:00-10:00
Interior Decoration II	W	7:00-10:00
Italian I and II	TuTh	7:00- 9:30
Japanese	MW	7:00- 9:00
Jewelry	W	6:30- 9:30
Life Science	MW	7:00-10:00
Mathematics—Basic	MW	7:00- 9:00
Medical Economics	M	7:00- 9:00
	Th	7:00- 9:00
Millinery I	Th	7:00-10:00
Photography I	M	7:00-10:00
Photography II	W	7:00-10:00
Photography III—Motion Picture Technique	M	7:00-10:00
Physical Education for Women	MW	7:00- 9:00
	TuTh	6:00- 8:00
	TuTh	8:00-10:00
Piano I	Tu	7:00-10:00
Piano II	Th	7:00-10:00
Piano III	F	7:00-10:00
Portrait Drawing and Painting	TuTh	7:00-10:00
Psychology of Personality	W	7:00- 9:30
Radio and Television	MW	7:00-10:00
Real Estate Law	Tu	7:00- 9:30
	Th	7:00- 9:30
Real Estate Appraisal	W	7:00- 9:30
Rugmaking—Beginning and Advanced	M	6:30- 9:30
Shorthand I and II—Gregg (two classes)	MWF	7:00- 9:00
Shorthand Speed Building	TuTh	6:30- 8:00
Shorthand III—Review, Gregg	TuTh	8:00- 9:30
Shorthand Dictation I	MW	7:00- 8:00
Shorthand Dictation II	MW	8:00- 9:00
Singing Fundamentals	F	7:00-10:00
Spanish I	MW	7:00- 9:00
	TuTh	6:30- 8:00
Spanish II	Tu	7:00- 9:00
	TuTh	8:00- 9:30
Spanish III and IV	MW	7:00- 9:00

Subject	Days	Hours
Typing—Beginning	MW	5:00– 7:00
	TuTh	5:00– 7:00
	MW	7:00– 9:00
	TuTh	7:00– 9:00
Typing—Mixed	MW	5:00– 7:00
	TuTh	5:00– 7:00
	MW	7:00– 9:00
	TuTh	7:00– 9:00
Upholstery	M	7:00–10:00
	Tu	7:00–10:00
	Th	7:00–10:00
	F	7:00–10:00
U.S. History I	W	6:30– 9:30
U.S. History II	F	6:30– 9:30
Vocational Floral Design and Construction	Tu	7:00–10:00

Schedule of Day Classes

Subject	Days	Hours
Clothing Construction		
Grant	W	9:00–12:00
Los Felis	F	9:00–12:00
Van Ness	Th	9:00–12:00
Vine	W	9:00–12:00
English IV—Vocabulary and Appreciation of Literature		
Hollywood Branch Library	F	1:00– 4:00
English V—Commercial Writing		
Hollywood Branch Library	T	1:00– 4:00
Home Decoration 1—Copper and Leather		
Alexandria	M	9:00–12:00
Van Ness	W	9:00–12:00
Home Decoration II—Ceramics		
Hollywood High School	MWF	1:00– 4:00
Millinery I		
Alexandria	Tu or W	9:00–12:00
Grant	Tu or Th	9:00– 1:00
Los Felis	M	9:00–12:00
Van Ness	F	9:00– 1:00
Parent Education—Discussion—Child Observation		
Griffith Park	W or F	9:45– 2:15
Los Felis	F	9:00–12:00
Ramona	Th	9:00–12:00
LeConte	Tu	9:30–11:30
Physical Education for Women		
Hollywood Congregational Church	MTh	8:30–10:30
Rugmaking		
Alexandria	Th	9:00–12:00
Spanish I		
Plummer Park	W	9:00–11:00

Subject	Days	Hours
Spanish II and III		
Plummer Park	MF	1:00- 4:00
Upholstery		
Hollywood High	M or Tu	9:00-12:00
Woodcarving		
Vine	Th	9:00-12:00

JORDAN ADULT SCHOOL, 1952-53
(Smallest Adult School in Los Angeles)
Schedule of Evening Classes

Subject	Days	Hours
Algebra	Tu	6:30- 9:30
Auto Body and Fender Repair	TuTh	7:00- 9:30
Chorus	Th	7:00- 9:30
Civics and Citizenship	Tu	6:30- 9:30
Civil Service Preparation	MW	7:00- 9:00
Clothing Construction I	MW, Tu, or F	6:30- 9:30
Clothing Construction II	Th	6:30- 9:30
Counseling	M	6:30- 9:30
Elementary Review		
(Grades 1 through 8)	MW or TuTh	6:30- 9:30
English	MW	6:30- 9:30
Foods I	MW	7:00- 9:00
Geometry	Tu	6:30- 9:30
History, U.S.	Th	6:30- 9:30
Home Decoration IV	F	6:30- 9:30
Mathematics	Tu	6:30- 9:30
Millinery I	M	6:30- 9:30
Office Practice	MW	7:00- 9:00
Orchestra	M	7:00- 9:30
Personal Grooming	MW	6:30- 9:30
Piano	Tu	7:00- 9:30
Practical Nursing	Tu	6:30- 9:30
Public Speaking	MW	6:30- 9:30
Spanish (Conversation)	Tu	7:30- 9:30
Textile Arts	W	6:30- 9:30
Typing	MTuWThF	6:30- 9:30
Upholstery	M	6:30- 9:30
Woodshop and Cabinetmaking	TuTh	7:00- 9:30

Schedule of Day Classes

Subject	Days	Hours
Clothing Construction I and II		
92nd Street School	Th	9:00-12:00
96th Street School	Tu	9:00- 1:30
111th Street School	M	9:00-12:00
Grape Street School	Th	9:30-12:30

Subject	Days	Hours
Will Rogers Park	W	9:00–12:00
Consumer Education		
Hacienda Village	MTuWThF	1:00– 3:30
Millinery		
Grape Street School	Tu	9:00– 1:30

APPENDIX VII

THE PROBLEM OF COURSE CLASSIFICATION

Course titles, a seemingly trivial matter, present an interesting dilemma for adult-school administrators. The schools can be related to their clienteles most expeditiously and effectively by titles that accurately describe course contents. A course wherein the teacher is to show films on American national parks has most appeal and most accurately selects its clientele if the title is specific, instead of "History and Travel." There has been a strong tendency for the schools to use popular descriptive titles, on the grounds of appeal and administrative convenience. Some descriptive titles have been troublemakers, however. They have drawn attention to subjects and practices of low acceptability and have aroused the wrath of state

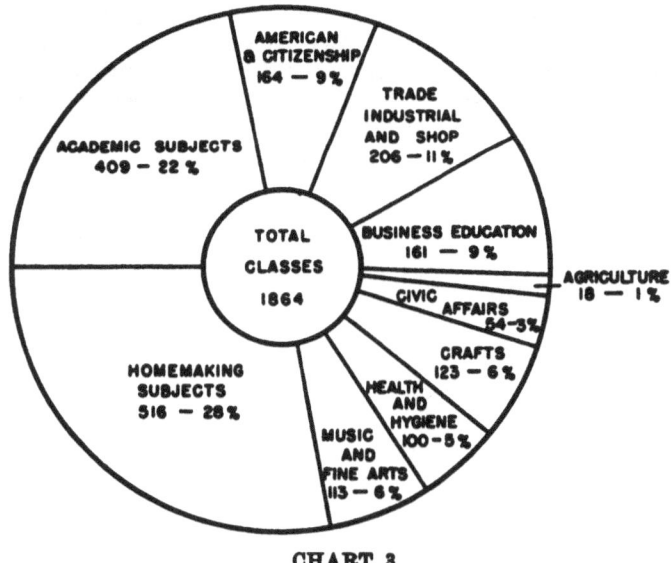

CHART 3

DISTRIBUTION OF CLASSES FOR ADULTS ASSIGNED BY SUBJECT FIELDS, LOS ANGELES CITY SCHOOLS, SCHOOL YEAR 1951–52 AS OF SIXTH SCHOOL MONTH, 1952

legislators, interest groups, and other educators. In self-protection, the administrators substitute nondescriptive, acceptable titles. "Cake-decorating" becomes "Foods and Nutrition," and "Floral Arrangements" becomes "Homemaking V." It is difficult to ascertain the precise composition of programs, for titles are often vague or misleading. Particularly in formal public reports, a wide range of courses is assimilated into traditional categories.

A typical graphic presentation of the schools is presented above, with subject-matter areas indicated by the percentage of classes falling in each. This is a breakdown from a January, 1953, report prepared by the Los Angeles administrators. The difficulty of giving real meaning to this classification is apparent in the following examples: photography classes are under "Trade and Technical"; home gardening is under "Agriculture"; driver education, police training, and civilian defense are "Civic Affairs"; wood carving and textile painting are "Crafts"; leather tooling, copper shaping, and clay work are "Homemaking." The formal categories are so difficult to interpret that an observer would need to visit a large number of the 1,800 classes in order to determine the actual program content. In addition, the formal classifications are stated by number of classes, rather than in units of enrollment or attendance size. However, the classes vary considerably in size, and the popular subjects provide the large enrollments. Classes clearly identified in the mail questionnaire as physical education (a troublesome category that has more and more come under state regulation) averaged over 70 in enrollment; homemaking classes (sewing, rugmaking, millinery, etc.) averaged 40; classes in vocational subjects, mathematics, and physical science averaged only 25 in enrollment. Thus the various formal categories have differential weightings in the enrollment economy.

This study has given little attention to the formal categories within which classes are reported, simply because they cannot be reliably interpreted. It is apparent that for programs of heterogeneous nature, many different classifications could be constructed. Administrators classify to present as favorable an impression as possible, and program critics classify unfavorably.

APPENDIX VIII

ORGANIZATIONS COSPONSORING ADULT CLASSES

This partial state-wide list for 1948-49 is taken from Philip M. Ferguson's unpublished dissertation (p. 72). The list is a mixture of specific organizations and types of organizations, but it serves the purpose of illustrating the wide range of cosponsoring organizations.

American Association of University Women
American Federation of Labor
American Institute of Banking
American Legion
Apprenticeship Council
Boy Scouts
Business Planning Institute
Business and Professional Women's Club
California Institution for Men
California State Prison
Chamber of Commerce
Chartered Life Underwriters
City Council
City Health Department
Coast Guard Auxiliary
Columbia Steel
Community Center
Community Social Betterment Association
Community Theater
Coördinating Council
County Apprenticeship Commission
County Architects Association
County Fish and Game Commission
County Superintendent of Schools
Dairy Institute
Daughters of American Republic
Department of Distributive Education
East Bay Church Federation
Electrical Bureau
Electrical Workers Union
Elementary Schools
Federal Union
Federation of Women's Clubs
Filipino Family Club
Fire Department
Folk Dancing Federation
Garden Club
Girl Scouts
Grange Association
Lockheed Aircraft Manufacturing Co.
Los Abiladores
Los Angeles City Jail
Los Angeles County Building Department
Los Angeles County Jail
Los Angeles County Sheriff's Reserve Corps
Los Angeles Park Department
Merchants Association
Mexican American Improvement Association
Ministerial Union
Mormon Church
National Electrical Contractors Association
Native Daughters of California
North American Aviation
Oil Drillers Association
Pacific Electric Railway
Pacific Telephone Employees Association
Parent-teacher associations
Pets and Pals Club
Pittsburgh Des Moines Steel Co.
Plasterers Union
Plumbers Union
Police Bureau
Public Library
Public Markets Association
Radio Amateurs Club
Real Estate Association
Recreation Department
Red Cross
Reedley Flight Club
Society of Friends
Stanislaus County Hospital
State Highway Commission
State Highway Patrol
Symphony Association
Toastmasters Club
UNESCO

U. S. Air Forces Procurement Office
U. S. Air Force Reserve
U. S. Army
U. S. Bureau of Immigration
U. S. Naval Reserve
U. S. Navy
Veterans Administration
Women's City Club
Y.M.C.A.

Appendix IX

FORM LETTER USED BY A COSPONSORING ORGANIZATION IN CONTACTING CLIENTELE

MEDICAL ASSISTANTS' ASSOCIATION
6253 Hollywood Blvd., Suite 1200
Hollywood 28, Calif.
Hollywood 9-3161

January 5, 1953

Dear Doctor and Assistant:

You will be interested in the enclosed announcement. It is about a series of courses designed to help doctors and their assistants.

The courses are sponsored by the Medical Assistants' Association and Los Angeles City Adult Schools. They are approved by the Los Angeles County Medical Association.

The purposes of the courses are:
1. To help medical assistants increase their knowledge of their own and their doctor's profession.
2. To raise the medical assistants' standards.
3. To provide a better knowledge of the basic principles of human and public relations.
4. To further knowledge and ability by discussion and exchange of ideas.

These classes will be given at the following schools:

Credit and Collections
    Monday, January 12, 7:00–9:00 p.m.
    Hollywood Adult School,
    1521 North Highland Avenue
    HOllywood 9-8668

Medical Office Management
    Tuesday, January 13, 7:00–9:00 p.m.
    Roosevelt Adult School,
    450 South Fickett Street
    ANgelus 9-4300

Medical Insurance
    Monday, January 12, 7:00–9:00 p.m.
    Van Nuys Adult School,
    6535 Cedros Avenue
    STate 5-5427

Enrollment will necessarily be limited, so may we suggest you insure your place in the class by calling the school where you wish to enroll.

Sincerely yours,
Signed: June Carroll
June Carroll, President
Medical Assistants' Association

Appendix X

EXCERPT FROM A CATALOGUE
EAST LOS ANGELES JUNIOR COLLEGE, 1952–53
(An example of branch organization of a community college)

The development of East Los Angeles Junior College into a real community college was given added impetus during the school year of 1951–52. The Branch that had been established at the City Hall in February, 1948, was expanded to include classes at the Department of Water and Power, Central Police Station, and the Police Traffic Building. The program which had been established in coöperation with the Los Angeles County Civil Service Commission was, during the year 1950–51, combined with the program at the City Hall to form a new, larger, and more effective Government Branch of the college. Also, the program at the Los Angeles County General Hospital was expanded to include additional offerings for graduate nurses, student nurses, practical nurses, attendants, and a refresher course for graduate nurses who felt the need for more up-to-date training. The following is a complete listing of all branch locations at East Los Angeles Junior College: Los Angeles County Civil Service Building, Los Angeles County Forestry Building, Los Angeles County General Hospital, Los Angeles City Hall, Los Angeles Department of Water and Power (Main Office, Washington Building, and Wright and Callender Building), Los Angeles Central Police Station, Los Angeles Traffic Headquarters Building, Collector of Internal Revenue, California Teachers' Association, California Hospital, Good Samaritan Hospital, State Highway Department, Chelf Army Air Force Specialized Depot, Methodist Hospital, Huntington Park High School, Roosevelt High School, Garfield High School, Los Angeles City Board of Education (Central Office and Business Office), Southern California Gas Company, Pacific Telephone and Telegraph Company.

Source: School Publication No. 542, Vol. VIII, No. 1, Los Angeles City Schools, p. 24.

Note: Most branches offer within-service training for the employees of the "host" agency.

BIBLIOGRAPHY

BIBLIOGRAPHY

SOURCES AVAILABLE FOR PUBLIC CIRCULATION

Almond, Gabriel A. *The American People and Foreign Policy*. New York: Harcourt, Brace and Co., 1950.
Barnard, Chester I. *The Functions of the Executive*. Cambridge: Harvard University Press, 1953.
Bennett, John W., and Melvin M. Tumin. *Social Life*. New York: Alfred A. Knopf, 1949.
Bogue, Jesse P. *The Community College*. New York: McGraw-Hill Book Co., 1950.
Bryson, Lyman. *A State Plan for Adult Education*. New York: American Association for Adult Education, 1934.
California. *Administrative Code*. Sacramento, 1951.
California. *Amendments to the School Law*. Sacramento, 1921.
California. Committee on the Conduct of the Study of Higher Education in California. *A Report of a Survey of the Needs of California in Higher Education*. 1948.
California. Department of Education. *Thirty-first Biennial Report*. Sacramento, 1924.
California. Department of Education. *Thirty-second Biennial Report*. Sacramento, 1926.
California. Department of Education. *Thirty-third Biennial Report*. Sacramento, 1928.
California. Department of Education. *Biennial Report, 1932*. Sacramento, 1932.
California. Department of Education. *Bulletin*, 1 (February, 1932). Sacramento, 1932.
California. Department of Education. *Bulletin*, 18 (May, 1949). Sacramento, 1949.
California. Department of Education. *Bulletin*, 20 (May, 1951). Sacramento, 1951.
California. Department of Education. Bureau of Adult Education. *Report and Proceedings, Adult Education Workshop*. 1949.
California. Department of Education. Bureau of Adult Education. *Report and Proceedings of the Montecito Workshop in Adult Education*. 1952.
California. *Education Code*. Sacramento, 1953.
California. Legislature. Senate. *Partial Report of the Senate Interim Committee on Adult Education*. Sacramento, 1953.
California Congress of Parents and Teachers, Inc. *Parent Education Manual, 1952-53*. Los Angeles, 1953.
California Schools, 22, no. 11 (November, 1951). Sacramento, 1951.
Cartwright, Morse A. *Ten Years of Adult Education*. New York: The Macmillan Co., 1935.
Cogan, Morris L. "Toward a Definition of Profession," *Harvard Educational Review*, 23 (1953), 33-50.
Conrad, Richard. "The Administrative Role: A Sociological Study of Leadership in a Public School System." Unpublished Ph.D. dissertation, Stanford University, 1951.
Cornell, Francis G. "Administrative Organization as Social Structure," *Progressive Education*, 30, no. 2 (November, 1952), 29-35.

Crawford, Will C. "Purposes and Personnel Administration of Adult Education." Unpublished Ed.D. dissertation, University of Southern California, 1939.

Danton, Emily M. "The Federal Emergency Adult Education Program," in D. Rowden, ed., *Handbook of Adult Education in the United States*. New York: American Association for Adult Education, 1936.

Debatin, Frank M. *Administration of Adult Education*. New York: American Book Co., 1938.

Education for All American Youth. Washington, D.C.: National Education Association of the United States, 1944.

Evans, E. Manfred. "Adult Education in Los Angeles City Schools, 1948–49," *New Los Angeles School Journal*, 32, no. 3 (October 18, 1948).

Ferguson, Philip M. "Practices in the Administration of Adult Education in the Public Schools of California." Unpublished Ed.D. dissertation, Stanford University, 1951.

Foote, Nelson N. "The Professionalization of Labor in Detroit," *American Journal of Sociology*, 58, no. 4 (January, 1953), 371–380.

Getsinger, Joseph W. "The History of Adult Education in the Public Schools of California." Unpublished Ed.D. dissertation, Stanford University, 1948.

Gouldner, Alvin W. *Patterns of Industrial Bureaucracy*. Glencoe, Illinois: The Free Press, 1954.

Hardin, Charles M. *The Politics of Agriculture*. Glencoe, Illinois: The Free Press, 1952.

Hathaway, William R. "Distributive Education—Economic Necessity," *Los Angeles School Journal*, 26, no. 5 (January 14, 1953).

Hendrickson, Andrew. *Trends in Public School Adult Education in Cities of the United States, 1929–1939*. New York: Teachers College, Columbia University, 1943.

Hertzler, Joyce O. *Society in Action*. New York: The Dryden Press, 1954.

Hofstadter, Richard, and C. DeWitt Hardy. *The Development and Scope of Higher Education in the United States*. New York: Columbia University Press, 1952.

Hunter, Guy. *Residential Colleges: Some New Developments in British Adult Education*. Occasional Papers no. 1. Pasadena, California: The Fund for Adult Education, n.d.

Kempfer, Homer. "State Programs of General Adult Education," *Adult Education Journal*, 7 (April, 1948), 75–81.

Lerner, Daniel, and Harold D. Lasswell, eds. *The Policy Sciences: Recent Developments in Scope and Method*. Stanford, California: Stanford University Press, 1951.

Los Angeles. Board of Education. *Controller's Annual Financial Report for the Fiscal Year Ending June 30, 1953*. Los Angeles, 1953.

Los Angeles City School Districts. *Expenditures Classified by Schools, School Year 1952–53*. Los Angeles, 1953.

Los Angeles City School Districts. Office of Public Information. *Saludos Amigos*. Los Angeles, 1952.

Los Angeles City School Districts. *Point of View*. Publication no. 470. Los Angeles, 1949.

Los Angeles City School Districts. *Self Realization through Adult Education*. Los Angeles, n.d.

MacIver, R. M., and Charles H. Page. *Society*. New York: Rinehart and Co., Inc., 1949.
MacKaye, David L. "Aims and Purposes of Adult Education in California," *Adult Education Bulletin*, 9 (October, 1944), 11-12.
MacKaye, David L. "Problems Underlying the Administration of Adult Education in California." Unpublished M.A. thesis, Stanford University, 1932.
Mannheim, Karl. *Freedom, Power, and Democratic Planning*. London: Routledge and Kegan Paul, 1951.
Meilandt, Ruth E. *A Study of the Adult Education Program of the Los Angeles City High School District*. Los Angeles: Chamber of Commerce, 1938.
Merton, Robert K. *Social Theory and Social Structure*. Glencoe, Illinois: The Free Press, 1949.
Merton, Robert K., et al., eds. *Reader in Bureaucracy*. Glencoe, Illinois: The Free Press, 1952.
Parsons, Talcott. *The Social System*. Glencoe, Illinois: The Free Press, 1951.
Riesman, David. *The Lonely Crowd*. New Haven: Yale University Press, 1950.
Roethlisberger, F. J., and William J. Dickson. *Management and the Worker*. Cambridge: Harvard University Press, 1950.
Ross, Arthur M. *Trade Union Wage Policy*. Berkeley and Los Angeles: University of California Press, 1950.
Sears, Jesse B. *Public School Administration*. New York: Ronald Press Co., 1947.
Selznick, Philip. "Foundations of the Theory of Organization," *American Sociological Review*, 13 (1948), 25-35.
Selznick, Philip. *Leadership in Administration*. Evanston: Row, Peterson and Co., 1957.
Selznick, Philip. *The Organizational Weapon*. New York: McGraw-Hill Book Co., 1952.
Selznick, Philip. *TVA and the Grass Roots*. Berkeley and Los Angeles: University of California Press, 1949.
Simon, Herbert A., D. W. Smithburg, and V. A. Thompson. *Public Administration*. New York: Alfred A. Knopf, 1950.
U.S. Bureau of the Census. *Statistical Abstract of the United States, 1953*. Washington, D.C.: U.S. Government Printing Office.
Veblen, Thorstein. *The Higher Learning in America*. Stanford, California: Academic Reprints, 1954.
Weber, Max. *The Theory of Social and Economic Organization*. Trans. A. M. Henderson and Talcott Parsons. New York: Oxford University Press, 1947.
Williams, Robin M., Jr. "Application of Research to Practice in Inter-Group Relations," *American Sociological Review*, 18 (February, 1953), 78-83.
Woofter, T. J., Jr. "The Status of Racial and Ethnic Groups," in *Recent Social Trends in the United States*. New York: McGraw-Hill Book Co., 1934.
Worthy, James E. "Organizational Structure and Employe Morale," *American Sociological Review*, 15 (April, 1950), 169-179.

INDEX

INDEX

Adaptation, organizational, 43–44. *See also* Clientele

Administrative staff: authority of, 105–106; defense against legislative inquiry, 126–128; duties of, 107; objectives, 63–65, 145–148, 157 ff.; other-directed orientation of, 106–108; part-time work of, 58; social structure of, 108–109

Adult education: Bureau of, 50, 59, 63, 126–128; constitutional status of, in California, 58; in England, 162; history of, in California, 47–51; in Los Angeles, 67–140; origin of, 49–51

American Association for Adult Education, 50

Americanization and citizenship, 48–49, 52, 76

Appropriations, state: and enrollment, 52–56, 61 ff.; as incentive, 51 ff.; as index of marginality, 60. *See also* Financing

Attendance: as condition of administrative decision-making, 61–62; effects on policy and procedure, 72–122 *passim*; as unit of state aid, 54–56

Barnard, Chester I., 147
Bryson, Lyman, 50
Bureau of Adult Education (California), 50, 59, 63; changes in authority of, 126–127, 128

California Association for Adult Education, 50
California Association of Adult Education Administrators, 59, 63
California Congress of Parents and Teachers. *See* Parent teacher associations
California Teachers Association, 97, 128
Campion, Howard A., 70
Cartwright, Morse A., 96
Chamber of commerce as cosponsor, 113, 117–118
Change, social. *See* Institutional change
Class size policy: effect on adult program, 75–77; effect on clientele, 73 ff.; effect on teaching force, 88–89, 102–103
Classes: evaluation of, 83; modifications in, 80–82; procedures for initiation, 79–80

Clientele: as affected by small-class policy, 73 ff.; as affected by tuition policy, 77–79; organizational adaptation to, 62, 72 ff., 88–89, 105; organized groups as, 110–118; unorganized, 85–86

Community center, adult school as, 160–162

Community college: and adult school, 130–140; operating pressures, 132; as service agency, 131–137; traditional junior college programs, 130–131

Competition, effect of, 130–140
Continuation school, 47, 49
Coöptation, formal, 116
Cosponsorship, 110 ff.; long-term advantages of, 116–118
Counselors, 72, 100–101

Decentralization, 150–151
Depression, effect of, 142

Enrollment. *See* Attendance; Clientele
Evans, E. Manfred, 70–71
Evening school, 47–49, 52

Financing, adult school: effect of state equalization formula, 55–56; recommendation of study on, 159–160; state legislation in California, 51–56. *See also* Appropriations
Folk schools, adult schools as, 160–162
Formal structure: of adult education branch, 70–72; of Los Angeles school system, 66 ff.

Goals. *See* Purpose

Hunter, Guy, 162 n.

Immigrant education, 48–49, 52, 76
Institution: functions of, 143–144; integrity of, 155–159
Institutional change, 43, 143 ff.; administrative control over, 157–158; effect of administrative purpose upon, 145–148; effect of decentralization upon, 150–151; effect of marginality upon, 148–150; effect of professionalism upon, 151–153; generated by group needs, 155; situation-directed, 145–146

[201]

Junior college. *See* Community college

Leadership, institutional, 44, 157–159, 160–162
Legislation, state. *See* Appropriations; Financing
Legislature, state, attack upon adult education, 125–130
Legitimacy of adult education, 57 ff.; as affected by cosponsorship, 113; low-cost rationale, 118–119; problem of educational respectability, 123–130; public-demand rationale, 120–122; public relations rationale, 119–120; service rationale, 121–122
Los Angeles, adult schools in, 67–140
Los Angeles Evening School Principals' Association, 72, 77

Mannheim, Karl, 146
Marginality, 57 ff., 62; as affected by legislative inquiry, 124–130; as source of administrative insecurity, 59–60, 148–150; symptoms of, 58–60
Medical Assistants' Association as cosponsor, 112, 113–114
Motor Vehicles, Department of, as cosponsor, 113, 114, 115, 116

Needs, organizational: conflict of, 123–124; as shaped by competition from community colleges, 130–140; as shaped by enrollment economy, 61–62; as shaped by legislative inquiry, 125–130; as shaped by organizational marginality, 57–60, 62; as shaped by traditional ethics of education, 123–125

Objectives. *See* Purpose

Parent teacher associations as cosponsors, 112–113, 114–115
Personnel. *See* Administrative staff; Teaching force
Professional associations, 69 n.
Professionalism: in adult-school teaching, 96–98; effect of, on institutional change, 151–153

Purpose, administrative, 63 ff.; impact on decision-making, 64–65, 157 ff.; and institutional change, 145–148

Richardson, Ethel, 50

Science Research Associates, 108
Selznick, Philip, 43 n., 116 n., 155 n.
Senate Interim Committee on Adult Education, 125–130
Service: as adult school orientation, 45, 110–118, 145–146, 147; as community college orientation, 131–137; ideology of, 119–122; as public relations slogan, 110; unanticipated consequences, 138
Specialization: in adult school and in junior college, 138–139; by geographic area, 148; impact on institutional change, 147–148; of purpose, 147–148; recommendation of study on, 160–162
State aid. *See* Appropriations
Stoddard, Alexander J., 135
Students. *See* Clientele

Teaching force, 86 ff.; evaluation of, 89; identification with administrative purpose, 98; identification with peers, 98–101; identification with small-class policy, 102–103; leadership within, 104; length of experience, 91–92; multiple jobs, 93–95; part-time employment, 92–95; professionalism, 96–98; recruitment, 95; remuneration by wage rate, 97–98; selection procedure, 86–88; social structure, 93–95, 103–105; strength of work codes, 104–105; student control over, 88–89, 105; tenure, 89–91; turnover, 91; work incentives, 97–98
Tenure, 89–91
Tuition, 77–79

Vocational education, 48–49; in community college, 136–137; federal support for, 48 n.

World War II, effect of, 142

www.ingramcontent.com/pod-product-compliance
Lightning Source LLC
Chambersburg PA
CBHW021711230426
43668CB00008B/795